The Money Question
During Reconstruction

THE NORTON ESSAYS IN AMERICAN HISTORY

Under the general editorship of
HAROLD M. HYMAN
University of Illinois

EISENHOWER AND BERLIN, 1945: THE DECISION TO
HALT AT THE ELBE
Stephen E. Ambrose

THE MONEY QUESTION DURING RECONSTRUCTION
Walter T. K. Nugent

ANDREW JACKSON AND THE BANK WAR
Robert V. Remini

The Money Question During Reconstruction

Walter T. K. Nugent

New York   W · W · NORTON & COMPANY · INC ·

For Al and Anne

Contents

Acknowledgments

FOR substantial and necessary support in the preparation of this study, I am happy to thank the John Simon Guggenheim Memorial Foundation and the Indiana University Foundation.

For permission to quote from copyrighted material, I would like to thank the American Historical Association and Executive Secretary Paul L. Ward (Bray Hammond, "The North's Empty Purse, 1861–1862," *American Historical Review,* LXVII [October 1961]); The Johns Hopkins Press (Robert P. Sharkey, *Money, Class & Party,* 1959); the *Journal of American History* and Managing Editor Martin Ridge (Stanley Coben, "Northeastern Business and Radical Reconstruction: A Re-examination," *Mississippi Valley Historical Review,* XLVI [June 1959]); The Princeton University Press (Joseph La Palombara, *Interest Groups in Italian Politics,* 1964).

A Brief Glossary
of Terms

〰〰〰〰〰〰〰〰〰〰〰〰〰〰〰〰〰〰〰〰〰〰〰〰〰〰〰

Bullion—Refined metallic gold and silver; usually, stamped by a Mint to certify its fineness (i.e. purity).

Bullionism—In the context of the late nineteenth century, a monetary theory and consequent policy which demanded that currency be made of bullion or at the very least convertible into it, which implied that the monetary standard be gold and/or silver. In pre-nineteenth-century economic thought, a variant of mercantilism.

Contraction—Secretary of the Treasury McCulloch's policy, authorized by Congress in 1866 and rescinded in 1868, of taking greenbacks out of circulation as a method of bringing the United States back to specie payments (q.v.)

Currency—What most people call "money"; actually, only that kind of money that circulates publicly as legal tender (q.v.). In the United States during Reconstruction, currency included the notes of national banks, government-issued paper (not bearing interest) such as the greenbacks, fractional paper (below one dollar), certificates for gold or silver, and mint-issued coins.

Free banking—The contemporary term for a policy of relaxing the requirements for the establishment of national banks, and hence the issuing of national bank notes, so that any person or persons who could put up the necessary capital could get a charter; advocated most prominently by Midwesterners in the early and middle seventies.

Free silver—A policy whereby the Mint would coin without limit whatever silver was brought to it to be coined; the traditional U. S. policy, halted by the Coinage Act of 1873, restoration of which many people advocated thereafter, usually at the traditional ratio of "sixteen to one," i.e. sixteen units of silver being legally equivalent to one unit of gold.

Gold monometallism—The theory and/or policy of a monetary standard consisting solely of gold.

International bimetallism—The theory and/or policy of a monetary standard consisting of gold and silver, at a ratio agreed upon by international treaty; differed from gold monometallism (q.v.) in that silver would be a standard along with gold; differed from free silver (q.v.) in that the use of silver as a standard would not occur without international agreement, which would (it was hoped) prevent any one country or group of countries from being denuded of gold or silver should the world supply of one of the metals change drastically.

Legal tender—The quality by which a currency (q.v.), under force of public law, must be accepted, if tendered by a debtor, for the payment of a public or private debt.

Money—A circulating medium of exchange or standard of value; the term includes not only currency (paper or coin) but demand deposits in banks and certificates thereof, clearing house certificates, personal checks, etc.

Producer philosophy—A political-economic theory or, better, attitude, especially before 1873 in America, that gave primacy to the productive function of farmers, laborers, manufacturers and others rather than to existing wealth in the form, particularly, of bullion; it led to the advocacy, in monetary policy, of greenbacks or free silver, and was widely held in the United States in the nineteenth century.

Refunding—In the language of public policy of the period, the replacement of higher-interest, shorter-term U. S. government bonds issued during the Civil War emergency with new and, it was hoped, less onerous bonds; authorization for refunding was substantially achieved in the Funding Act of July 14, 1870.

Specie—Gold and silver coin, as distinct from metallic gold and silver.

Specie payments—The practice, customary in the United States before 1862 and after 1878, of banks and the Treasury to exchange specie for bank notes or greenbacks at the customer's demand.

The Money Question
During Reconstruction

1

Introduction: A Generation's Migraine

~~~~~~

ON WINGS OF INDIGNATION, the Vincent brothers, Harry and Will, flew from their erstwhile home in Iowa in the summer of 1886 and alighted at Winfield, a dusty south-central Kansas town not long out of the raw frontier. The Vincents' main cargo was a weekly newspaper which they and their father had published in Iowa for several years, and which, after touching ground in Winfield, they renamed *The American Nonconformist and Kansas Industrial Liberator*. Harry and Will's first Kansas issue of the *Noncon* hit the streets and the country post offices on October 7, 1886. Featured prominently was this item, aimed at the railroad magnate Jay Gould, but really a catalog of radical grievances that had accumulated for a decade:

Gould's Prayer

Our father who art in England, Rothschild be thy name, thy financial kingdom come to America, thy will be done in the United States as it is in England. Give us this day our bonds in gold, but not in silver; give us plenty of laboring men's votes to keep monopoly in power and its friends in office. We know, our father, we have done many things that were wrong; we have robbed the honest poor, and brought distress to many a door; we know it was wrong to refund the bonds and make them payable in coins. We know it was wrong to demonetize silver; we know it was wrong to water our railroad stocks; but thou knowest we made money by that. Now, our father, thou knowest we are above politics. It is the same to us whether the Democrats or Republicans rule, for thou knowest we are able to sway all political jobs in our favor. Lead us not into the way of the strikers, but deliver us from the hands of the insane Knights of Labor. Thus shall we have the kingdom of bonds, interests, powers and gold until the Republic shall end. Amen.

Such effusions became the Vincents' stock in trade, and a few months later they capped exhortation with action by traveling to Texas, getting themselves invested in the National Farmers' Alliance and Industrial Union (the "Southern Alliance"), and bringing the Alliance's methods and message back to Kansas. The result was the whirlwind spread of the Alliance throughout Kansas and neighboring states in 1889 and the founding of the People's Party at Topeka in June, 1890. By then the movement had grown completely beyond the Vincents' control. Combining with other grass-roots agrarian uprisings in the South and West, feeding on depression conditions, Populism fought the "old parties" on local, state, and national levels until in 1896 it fused with the rejuvenated national Democracy to fight the crusade for Bryan and free silver.

The spleens of editorialists like the Vincents demanded considerably more venting than those of their readers and the emerging mass of Populist voters. Nevertheless, there were hundreds of thousands of Americans still furious in the fall of 1896 at a government that they felt was not theirs. That government had sinned against them for thirty years. It had promised in March, 1869, so they said, to pay its towering Civil War debt in coin rather than in paper "greenbacks." It had legislated in July, 1870, to refund that debt into a long-term burden on the taxpayers, payable in coin, while simultaneously it passed another law limiting the circulation of greenbacks. It "surreptitiously" had put an end to the standard silver dollar in the Coinage Act of February 12, 1873—the "Crime of '73" —thus in effect re-defining "coin" as gold, and making the burden owed by the American taxpayers, heavier than ever. Shameful were the circumstances many believed to have surrounded the demonetization of silver—that it had resulted from the direct bribery of Congressmen by foreign investors (especially the Rothschilds) who stood most to benefit. Then in early 1875, Congress passed the Specie Resumption Act, which was effectuated within four years by Secretary of the Treasury John Sherman, deflating the currency of the country until it was at par with gold. If all this were not perfidy enough, greater shame showered on the government because of the privileged "monopoly" position these people felt it gave to the national banks, which drew interest in gold on the government bonds the banks bought, and interest a second time on the notes the banks were then empowered to create and lend.

By the mid-nineties, the legislative legacy of the Reconstruction Congresses and Administrations appeared to the Populists and Bryanites to have been legislation in the interest of a class, especially the Americans and foreigners who held the bonds and limited the currency of the country to gold and gold-convertible notes. Those that had, got; those that hadn't, paid. Bonds bought during the Civil War with paper were paid in gold —a tremendous windfall for the investor. Currency, needed to pay private debts as well as public, was getting scarcer year by year. Was pro-gold financial legislation inevitable? Was money (the equivalent of currency for many of these people) getting scarcer through some natural process only? It hardly seemed true. As the "bloated plutocrats" of "Gould's Prayer" confessed: "We know it was wrong. . . . we know it was wrong. . . . we have done many things that were wrong."

To a very large body of Americans in the mid-nineties, and for two decades before that, the money question was crucial. The quiet, recondite financial legislation of the Reconstruction period had revealed itself shamelessly for what it really was: conspiratorial robbery by class against mass. And it had been purposeful.

That "unresponsive" government in Washington, though it may have been far removed in many ways from the Winfield, Kansases, of the country, was nonetheless as occupied as they were with the money question through the whole post-1865 period. Little more than a year after the passage of the Specie Resumption Act in January, 1875, and well before it was implemented, Congressional members of both political parties began powerful drives to repeal not only that act but the 1873 demonetization of silver. Only twice in the next fifteen years were they successful at all, and both of these "victories"—the Bland-Allison Act of 1878 and the Sherman Silver Purchase

Act of 1890—provided only for rather limited purchasing and coining of silver by the government. They came nowhere near restoring the silver standard, or the greenback, or repealing specie resumption.

Then, in 1893, in response to yet another severe monetary crisis (which, like the one of 1873, heralded a full-scale depression), President Cleveland called Congress into special session to repeal one of those victories, the Act of 1890. This Congress did. But repeal came only after a revealing "great debate" on the whole history of the money question as it had developed since the late sixties. Some of the policy-makers of the Reconstruction period were still in public life, and participated in that debate. Though time sometimes played tricks with their memories, perspective (and the prodding of the other side) produced vigorous, forthright assertions of their motives of two decades earlier. Very simply, very basically, they had been and still were determined to maintain the public credit and the integrity of the currency: the watchword was "honest money". Why? Because the public interest, the national honor, required it. John Sherman of Ohio, the chief Republican financial legislator in 1893 just as he had been in 1873, vehemently declared this during the debate on the repeal of the Silver Purchase Act of 1890.

Was the demonetization of 1873 done surreptitiously? On behalf of a privileged few against the mass interest? "In every stage of the bill and every print[ing]," Sherman growled, "the dollar of 412½ grains was prohibited, and the single gold standard recognized, proclaimed, and understood. It was not until silver was a cheaper dollar that anyone demanded it, and then it was to take advantage of a creditor." [1] Earlier Sherman explained his profound opposition to free silver: "I was one of those who believed that [free silver] would be a very grave and serious peril to our country—not to one party, but to the whole country—that it would place us in a position to demonetize gold and adopt silver as the single standard, to detach ourselves from the great commercial nations of the world and join the

---

1. *Congressional Record*, XXV (August 30, 1893), p. 1061.

inferior nations, where poverty or large populations compel them to the use of silver alone." [2]

Another key participant in the 1873 silver demonetization was the then Secretary of the Treasury George S. Boutwell of Massachusetts. Boutwell, very much alive in 1893 and appealed to during the debate of that year by Senator Sherman and others, explained his actions forthrightly then and in his memoirs published a few years later. Surreptitious? Malfeasant?

In 1873 I had come to believe that it was wise for every nation to recognize, establish, and maintain the gold standard. I was of the opinion then, as I am of the opinion now, that nations cannot escape from the gold standard in all interstate transactions. . . . The *choice* of gold as the standard was not due to hostility to silver or to the silver mining interests, but to the well grounded opinion that gold was a universal currency, while in some countries, as in England or Germany, silver coins were not a debt-paying currency. . . . The measure was in accord with my policy, and it was in accord with the unbiased judgment of the commissions.[3]

Thus did the sides form in the great debate. The perpetrators of the Crime of '73, who had refinanced the Civil War debt in such a way as to fasten an immense burden on future tax-paying generations and at the same time had redefined the country's monetary standard so as to induce severe deflation, turned out to be the embattled guardians of the public honor and credit, striving to keep American finance on a respectable level among civilized nations. Conversely, the toiling masses, the farmers and laborers, the producers upon whose pure hearts and brawny shoulders the future of the country depended, were really trying to pull a gigantic confidence trick by which they would pay their own and the country's creditors in the debased and fraudulent currency of free silver.

2. *Ibid.,* (August 8, 1893), p. 216.
3. George S. Boutwell, *Reminiscences of Sixty Years in Public Affairs* (New York: McClure, Phillips & Co., 1902), II:151–52. "Commissions" referred to a body Boutwell appointed in 1869 within the Treasury to codify the coinage laws. It included Deputy Comptroller of the Currency John Jay Knox and former Director of the Mint Henry R. Linderman, and polled many officials and private persons on the coinage question.

Neither side was totally out of touch with reality. The country had to have credit, and in an age when a very substantial portion of the public bonds had to be sold on foreign markets, the intangible reality called investor confidence had to be guarded integrally, for it was crucial. On the other side, people did not join the Farmers' Alliance and the Populist party or vote for Bryan and free silver in 1896 because they were muckers or out for a cheap buck; nearly two-thirds of the American population was rural in 1890, and economic stringency among farmers was maddeningly real. The leading spokesmen on each side, moreover, repudiated the more extreme accusations that some of their own allies made. Though the Eastern press denounced free silver (as it had denounced greenbackism years before) as anarchy, communism, a criminal conspiracy hell-bent on destroying the Republic, Senator Sherman and other responsible leaders distinguished carefully between free-silver doctrine and the people who accepted it: hate the sin, but love the sinner. Though some Populist and other free-silver editorials screeched about the "Crime of '73" and bribery of Congress with English gold, though Mrs. Sarah E. V. Emery put the "Crime" among "seven conspiracies that shook the world" (all perpetrated by Civil War and Reconstruction Congresses), such Populist Congressmen as John Davis of Kansas and Senator Kyle of South Dakota, discarded the bribery-conspiracy aspect of the demonetization though they denounced the legislation itself and its effects.

Both sides in the great debate, of which the Congressional battle in 1893 over repeal of the Silver Purchase Act was a sort of preview and the national election campaign of 1896 the culmination, agreed that the money question was fundamental among the nation's problems. Both sides looked upon the money question not just as a matter of legislation, but far more importantly as a matter of public and private morality: was the country to conduct its affairs in an honorable manner or wasn't it? Was the government to respond in a republican way to the requirements of the people as a whole, or only to certain special and self-interested segments? If the latter, whoever the segments represented, it would be fundamentally at odds with itself—denying its past, and damning its future. Each side rooted its position in *some* of the economic and social realities, and by the time of the great debate of the nineties (in fact ever since the mid-seventies), each side propounded a line of argument, a rhetoric, that, taken alone, seemed virtually irrefutable.

But both sides were deluded. Both became hypnotized by money and their own rhetoric about it. Both believed a "proper" solution to the money question would bring "proper" solutions to the outstanding social and economic problems of the country and fasten upon the country a happy and moral future. Both made money the surrogate of social concern—not just once, but twice, in the final third of the nineteenth century. For the great debate of the nineties was in a large sense only the second act of a comic opera that had begun just after the Civil War and had reached its first-act intermission at the close of the seventies.

It was not a very good drama. The second act mostly repeated the first and, like it, ended in a stalemate. But no third act followed to resolve the issues cleanly. As early as the middle of the first act, by 1876, the characters were disclaiming at the audience, rather than communicating with each other. In fact the whole issue, the money question itself, now seems so tinny that a present-day audience has to marvel at how the whole post-Civil War generation could ever have let themselves become so fascinated with it.

Why did they? Why did they come out of the Civil War, quickly turn their backs on the great war-nurturing issues of racial and state-federal relations, avoid direct confrontations with such new postwar issues as the absorption of immigrants, the mushrooming of large businesses, the dissatisfaction of farmers, workers, and city-dwellers, the headlong growth of cities and the nationalization of so many aspects of life and, instead, concentrate on the money question? The country had just suffered a sectional war to get rid of slavery. Would it get through an industrial-urban revolution without a class war?

The money question became the substitute for these issues and, supposedly, the means by which to answer them. Convoluted states-rights arguments had become a gigantic euphemism for slavery before the war; convoluted monetary rhetoric became a surrogate for social problems after the war. No one realized it in 1865, but money was destined to become the chief perennial issue in national politics for over thirty years, reaching a culmination in the election of 1896 with William Jennings Bryan's campaign for free silver. Its peculiar dimensions were established in almost all important ways during the Reconstruction years, from 1867 to 1879.

The money question as it took shape in America during Reconstruction was the product of many forces. Among these forces were personalities and personal decisions; ideologies accepted and voiced by these personalities; economic conditions, not only in the United States but around the world; the dreams and plans of the great capitalistic nations; and the American Civil War. These several forces are the subjects of the next three chapters. After that, one can see how they flowed together to shape policy.

2

The Civil War and Its Unforeseen Legacies

THE CIVIL WAR of 1861-65 was the most shattering single event in the history of the United States. A brothers' war, it climaxed three decades of sectional antagonism, the ultimate roots of which were as ancient as English settlement in North America. It still ranks as by far the bloodiest and most devastating war, in percentages of casualties and men at arms to the whole population, in which the United States has ever been engaged. A Lockean "appeal to heaven", a constitutional argument of the last resort, it forever stilled claims of state sovereignty as a serious position and threw the balance of political power, though by no means all such power, to the central government. The federal Congress, freed by secession from stubborn Southern conservatism, passed a series of laws representing a spirit of economic activism and nationalization that was never again to be dissipated. Among these laws were the Homestead Act of 1862, giving away parcels of the public domain to persons who would settle on and cultivate them; the Pacific Railway Acts of 1862 and 1864, by which the federal government, in one of the greatest implementations of social overhead capital in modern history, subsidized by money and land grants the construction of a railroad across the North American continent; the Morrill Land Grant College Act of 1863, which provided federal aid for a revolutionary new kind of higher education; the Morrill Tariff Acts of 1861, 1862, and 1864, which permanently raised protective levels; and a whole series of financial laws. The causes of these initiatives were diverse. Long-standing sectional pressures, short-term electoral considerations, an ideological strain of central-government vigor going back to John Quincy Adams, Gallatin, Hamilton, and the mercantilism of an even earlier day, all played a part.

So did the immediate emergency of the war effort. The financial legislation, in particular, developed very largely out of the sheer critical need of the federal government to get the funds to pay for the war effort. Within weeks after the war began, the banks of the country were so short of gold and silver that they had to suspend the practice, traditionally a sign of banking solvency and probity, of paying specie for bank notes on a customer's demand. There was no federal deposit insurance in those days; hard money went into hiding. Nor was there an income tax, and although the government soon adopted one as a fund-raising expedient, it could not wholly solve the fund shortage. There was no central bank, like the Bank of England or the Banque de France, to mobilize and control the money resources of the country. The United States, astonishingly, limped along without a central bank for another fifty years until the creation of the Federal Reserve System on the eve of World War I.

The government had to raise vast sums in a hurry, and the prewar financial structures of the country were hopelessly inadequate, even obstructive. Congress solved the dilemma by adopting four measures. First, higher taxes were imposed, both direct internal ones and higher import duties (the new tariffs were devices for revenue as well as for protection). Secondly, authority was granted to the Treasury to borrow heavily by selling bonds. And borrow it did; by the end of the war this bonded debt, amounting to more than two billion dollars, was in the hands of creditors ranging all the way from the humbler of American farmers and artisans to the great merchant banks of England and continental Europe. Bond buyers could be anyone to whom the government's agents could sell the bonds quickly for cash, even paper cash, in return for later payment in, perhaps, gold. The third measure was nothing less than a whole new system of banks, federally chartered and regulated. These new "national banks" were partly an instrument for selling government bonds (since a sizable portion of a national bank's capital, in gold, had to be exchanged for bonds before the Treasury would grant a charter) and partly a device for relieving the currency shortage, since the national banks were given what amounted to exclusive power to issue bank currency, the "national bank notes," which they could lend to borrowers or pay to depositors or other banks in lieu of gold or silver. Fourthly, and only as a temporary expedient, the government itself was authorized by Congress to create and put in circulation a currency without precious-metal backing: the "legal-tender notes," or greenbacks. This measure was at the time the least liked by Congress (and many outsiders) and was the most radical in terms of traditional monetary theory and practice. Even its creators hoped it would rapidly disappear when the wartime financial emergency was over. The other measures were considered permanent by the Congresses that passed them; not so the greenbacks.[1]

That was war. What was "normalcy"?

Like many great events, the Civil War had an immediate aftermath that saw the war's most noble purposes treated with unseemly dispatch. But some of its accidental side-effects unexpectedly left a heavy and wearisome legacy. The ending of slavery, the integration of the ex-slaves into new economic and social patterns, and the resumption of what President Lincoln called the "proper practical relation" of the Confederate states to the Union, were clearly the major problems facing the country in the final phases of the war. The victorious Union did indeed deal with these problems after Appomattox, and tumultuously. It has all been well recorded and long debated—the story of Presidential Reconstruction under Andrew Johnson, the very different Reconstruction policy hammered out by Congress in 1866 and 1867, the impeachment of the President and the passage of the Fourteenth Amendment to the Federal Constitution in 1868. But there, as a question riveting the attention and

1. I have depended here on an authoritative recent discussion of early Civil War finance and the genesis of the greenbacks: Bray Hammond, "The North's Empty Purse, 1861–1862," *American Historical Review,* LXVII (October 1961), 1–18.

energies of the nation, Reconstruction ended. After 1868 came no more impeachments, no new policies, no ingenious efforts to replace slavery with a just and viable system of race relations. Congress and most of the nation were already looking elsewhere, and in the meantime the Reconstruction policy laid down by Congress in the Act of 1867 and its sequels devolved gradually into "normal" home rule. One by one the rebellious states crept back into a "proper practical relation" until the moribund program of Reconstruction finally died in 1877 with the exit of a few thousand Union troops from the last three occupied Southern states. The questions of Reconstruction, so burning for the three years from the spring of 1865 to the middle of 1868, no more carried emotional charges after that time than the fate of European democracy would concern America after 1920.

Other times, other problems. The questions that concerned people longest after the Civil War, much longer than Reconstruction policy itself, were the stubborn by-products of the financial emergency of the early war years that were to vex the country for more than a generation. In the postwar context of rapid demographic, economic, and social change, they took on an importance not guessed at in the early sixties and not by any means caused solely by the war itself, though the war was when they had begun.

At the very time that the radical Republicans in Congress were devising a Reconstruction policy, officials in the Treasury Department and the financial committees of Congress were facing up to the fiscal mess left by the War. Any return to normalcy in the area of national finance would have to involve an accommodation between long-standing pre-war practice and principles, and the new realities that stemmed from the war emergency.

Nearly everyone expected, and most people desired, a rapid return to the old practice of specie payments. Before 1861 the holder of a "money substitute," such as a bank note, expected to be able to convert it into "real money," i.e. gold or silver coin. In practice this meant gold, since silver had been so scarce since the late 1830's that it had almost disappeared from circulation. By the end of the war the notes of state and private banks had also generally disappeared because the National Banking Acts had taxed them out of existence in order to favor the establishment of the national banks as instruments of wartime finance. Postwar currency thus consisted for practical purposes of national bank notes and greenbacks: both paper, both "money substitutes" in pre-war terms. During the war the national bank notes and the greenbacks had been convertible with each other, but not nearly convertible with gold. Scarcer by far than the two paper currencies, yet still essential for certain important transactions (some taxes, import duties, and purchases from a foreign seller), gold could be bought with greenbacks only at a stiff premium over face value. At one point in 1864 it took over $2.50 in greenbacks to buy a dollar in gold and, even though such inflation had subsided by the time of the Union victory, the gold premium over greenbacks was still very considerable. The Treasury could hardly resume specie payments until this premium disappeared, or else people would naturally drain the Treasury and foolhardy banks of all the gold they had. It would have been disastrously simple: for example, if the gold premium happened to be 50 (i.e. $150 in greenbacks bought $100 in gold), anyone could have taken $150 in greenbacks to the Treasury, received $150 in gold, pocketed $50, sold the other $100 for a new $150 in greenbacks on the open market, taken the new $150 to the Treasury for another $150 in gold, pocketed another $50, and kept going until the gold was gone. Since thousands would have done the same thing, the Treasury and bank stocks of gold would have disappeared within days or hours. If the resumption of specie payments was not devised with extreme care, the country would have gone bankrupt in foreign exchange, because the government was obligated to pay its creditors (many of them foreign), and private businessmen their foreign creditors, in gold.

So the gold premium had to disappear and greenbacks brought into equilibrium with gold before resumption could take place. Johnson's Secretary of the Treasury, a former Indiana banker of hard-money Jacksonian beliefs named Hugh McCulloch, saw that the most direct route to equilibrium was to take a hefty share of the greenbacks out of circulation and at the same time build up the Treasury's stock of gold. This road to resumption was called "contraction" (of the greenbacks), and it proved too rocky for nearly everyone except McCulloch. In early 1868, Congress rescinded the authority it had given Secretary McCulloch two years earlier, and which he had been using, to contract the greenbacks. Postwar deflation had set in at about the time McCulloch started contracting, and his policy seemed to be intensifying a tight-money trend that bore heavily on a wide spectrum of economic interest groups. McCulloch regretfully acquiesced in the Congressional decision to postpone rapid resumption in order to avert a further slide into depression. But though the contraction policy stopped, the resumption ideal assuredly did not: as the New York *Commercial and Financial Chronicle* insisted in an editorial of August 29, 1868, "A little reflection upon the gains and losses to which we have referred [how the gold premium affected various groups], is sufficient to convince any intelligent mind, that under an irredeemable and depreciated currency the whole trade and industry of the country is in a perturbed and unnatural condition; the fluctuations in gold so affecting values that chance reigns instead of law, chaos instead of order."

Another factor made McCulloch's contraction policy extremely difficult to execute successfully. This factor was an offshoot of a second troublesome financial legacy of the war, the bonded debt. The national debt was figured in mid-1866 at more than $2.8 billion, which included about $1.2 billion of "debt bearing coin interest," a similar amount "bearing currency interest," and about $400 million in greenbacks, the "non-interest-bearing debt." At the same time that he was trying to accumulate gold for specie resumption, McCulloch had to sell gold on the open market through the Subtreasury in New York, partly in order to help keep the gold premium down, and partly in order to buy the government's own bonds in sufficient quantity to keep their prices—which meant the national credit rating—at a stable and respectable level.

The most dramatic example of this policy of selling gold occurred at the time of the brief but severe Overend, Gurney

Panic in England in 1866. In the classic pattern of a financial panic, the failure of the important London financial institution of Overend, Gurney brought a sharp and sudden demand for liquid funds by other institutions who feared or actually faced demands by their creditors for payment of short-term debts. One likely source of such liquid funds was from the quick sale of American bonds. Shiploads of them arrived in New York to be sold. McCulloch could have left the bond market alone, allowed the bond sellers to take what low prices they could find, and thus have watched the ruin of many foreign bondholders and the enrichment of many domestic ones. He preferred to intervene. He authorized the sale of millions in Treasury gold at a below-market price, thus liquefying the New York (and London) financial markets and keeping the gold premium and the price of American government bonds reasonably steady. Some Wall Streeters grieved that McCulloch's intervention "unquestionably saved the Bank of England from suspension" and prevented a process that would have made New York, rather than London, "the principal financial city of the world." [2] But McCulloch defended his gold sales as in the interests of the "laboring and producing classes," who depended utterly on "the general steadiness of the market, the gradual advance of currency toward the true standard of value, and the prevention of financial troubles." [3]

In addition to hindering specie resumption, the huge debt carried cruel interest rates that had been the best the government thought it could get during wartime. Awesome quantities of the bonds would soon be redeemable. Nearly everyone in a position to influence policy believed it was absolutely crucial to keep up confidence in the public credit, which meant not only keeping the market prices of the bonds fairly stable, but also meeting the interest and principal as they came due. These were laudable purposes, but the sheer size and imminence of the debt threatened the public credit constantly. To policy-

2. James K. Medberry, *Men and Mysteries of Wall Street* (Boston: Fields, Osgood, & Co., 1870), p. 257.
3. McCulloch to House Speaker Schuyler Colfax, open letter in *Bankers' Magazine* (New York), July 1866.

makers like Secretary McCulloch and Senator John Sherman, who was Chairman of the Senate Finance Committee through this period, the interest-bearing debt had to be renegotiated at better rates and, at the same time, the confidence of investors and the equities of creditors had to be protected zealously. Therefore for several years after 1867, Senator Sherman and successive Treasury Secretaries worked for legislation that had the dual effect, as seen in retrospect, of spreading the debt over a longer payment period at lower rates, but also of increasing considerably the total amount payable. The wartime acts of Congress authorizing the various bond issues were not always very clear about the way in which the bonds were to be repaid; some specified "coin," but others could be and were construed as payable in "lawful money," meaning greenbacks. With rapid specie resumption out of the picture by early 1868, when Congress terminated McCulloch's contraction authority and put no other resumption policy in its place, many bonds payable in the near future could be paid in "depreciated greenbacks," which Sherman and many others felt would constitute a "repudiation" of the government's obligation.

As soon as the Grant administration took office in March, 1869, Congress passed a "Public Credit Act" declaring "that the faith of the United States is solemnly pledged to the payment in coin or its equivalent of all the obligations of the United States" except for debts "expressly provided" in the authorizing law as payable in "lawful money or other currency than gold and silver." In July, 1870, after much debate, Congress effectuated this declaration of intent and at the same time resolved the debt problem by passing "an act to authorize the refunding of the national debt." Civil War bonds outstanding at five and six percent could thence be exchanged, par for par, for new bonds of $50 or more, "redeemable in coin of the present standard value." Some of the new bonds were payable in ten years and bore 5 percent interest; others were fifteen-year bonds at 4.5 percent; but two-thirds of them were payable in thirty years and carried 4 percent. All were completely tax-exempt. The public credit was protected. But it was also true that bonds bought with greenbacks during the war would ultimately be paid in gold earned by taxpayers for the rest of the century.

The war, in addition to leaving the problems of specie resumption and the public credit, disordered the currency and money system of the country. Legally and traditionally, the United States had a double monetary standard of gold and silver, with the ratio between them set by law at one unit of gold to sixteen units of silver. In practice, as we have seen the currency of the country had consisted for decades of gold and paper and gold had sold at a premium, paper at a discount. To get rid of the premium-discount situation was to create the essential condition for resuming specie payments.

But achieving this was not going to be easy, as McCulloch's short-lived contraction policy showed. In the years following the war, policy-makers at the Treasury (though by no means everyone in Congress) looked forward yearningly to resumption day, but they were forced to be content with a very gradual build-up of Treasury gold reserves while doing nothing more vigorous with regard to the greenbacks than avoiding increasing the amount already in circulation. Eventually, they hoped, the economy would simply keep growing until demands for greenbacks to conduct commerce would raise the price of them to par with gold.

The Treasury gold reserve could not really rise without the help of two factors: stable public credit and a favorable balance of trade. And these factors did come to exist during the seventies. The refunding of the debt along the lines of the Act of July, 1870, went slowly but successfully—so successfully, in fact, that John Sherman, who took a vacation from the Senate to become Secretary of the Treasury for a few years during the Hayes administration, was actually able to sell more bonds for gold in the late seventies. At the same time, in a stroke of blind luck for those striving for resumption, the country enjoyed a favorable trade balance and a net increase in its gold stock. Resumption day passed without a ripple on January 2, 1879. The greenbacks, the national bank notes, and gold were at par and convertible; the United States was on the gold standard externally and internally.

But a great many people were very unhappy that this was

so. As the resumption process went on, other things happened to the money of the country that met with less than universal applause. In the first place, the national banking system disturbed many people because of the way in which it had been administered. The total sum of national bank-note currency was limited by law, and the Treasury issued charters during the war to people with the capital to set up such banks on a first-come, first-served basis. Naturally the banks concentrated heavily in New England and the Middle Atlantic states. The capital-shy Middle West and South thus became even more currency-hungry in relation to the Northeast. Western Congressmen and Senators exerted strong pressure to get the national banking system expanded, and succeeded only in 1875, when the Specie Resumption Act included a provision for the unrestricted formation of national banks (and hence their notes, which were to replace greenbacks up to a certain point). Still, the national banking system tended to favor the Northeast in financial resources over the less developed sections.

Another source of sectional monetary imbalance was related to this maldistribution. In the theorizing of greenbackers the term "money" often meant "currency." The postwar years saw a tremendous development in the United States of forms of money other than currency; foremost among these were deposits in commercial and savings banks. The amount of currency dollars in 1867 was only slightly smaller than the amount of bank-deposit dollars, but because of the remarkable growth of banking in the next five years, deposit dollars were double the amount of currency dollars just before financial panic occurred in 1873.[4]

There was even more to it than that. Bank deposits were situated, of course, in banks; places that had banks had a much more plentiful money supply. Also, the Northeast with its shorter distances and greater density of banks benefited from a substantially greater amount of available money and also from

4. Milton Friedman and Anna Jacobson Schwartz, *A Monetary History of the United States, 1867–1960* (Princeton: Published by Princeton University Press for the National Bureau of Economic Research, Inc., 1963), p. 16.

a much more rapid flow of it: not only did it possess a heavy share of the money supply, but it could employ its money at a higher velocity than could other parts of the country. As Senator Oliver Morton, the Indiana Republican and leading spokesman for "free banking," pointed out during the 1870 debate on the expansion of the national banks, "The ten-dollar bill which is used in a county in Iowa will not change hands half a dozen times while the same ten-dollar bill would change hands a hundred times in Massachusetts or in London." [5] But few heard him. Add to this the increasing use of credit instruments in major centers, such as certificates issued by the New York Clearing House Association to facilitate inter-bank exchanges, and soon, even to make loans to its members, and one arrives at a picture of the Northeast increasingly independent of actual currency issues, while other sections of the country remained largely ignorant of these modern monetary developments and scarcely aware that any form of money existed except currency itself.

Something else happened during the period that did not immediately affect the money supply of the country, but that had profound political and currency implications: the demonetization of silver. Just as the monetary legacies of the Civil War were a relatively minor by-product of the war emergency itself, so the silver legislation of 1873 was almost a detail amid the great problems of specie resumption, debt refunding, and currency stabilization. But in a very few years it would outrun them all in political importance. Man proposed, but God (or fate) disposed; the incidental became central. The silver dollar had been established as the legal monetary unit of the United States in 1792. The gold dollar had at first been measured in terms of it. During the Jackson administration, with some of the fiscal innocence that prevailed so generally in the Executive Branch in those days, the government changed the gold dollar slightly to create the one-to-sixteen ratio—with the result that, since an ounce of silver was worth more on the open market than one-sixteenth of an ounce of gold, silver began disappearing from circulation. After gold became increasingly plentiful

5. *Congressional Globe,* 41 Cong. 2 Sess., p. 733.

the world over when it was discovered in Australia and California in the late forties, the disappearance of silver became virtually complete. Congress passed a coinage law in 1853 which debased the "minor coinage"—silver coins of denominations below the dollar—and thereby kept them in circulation because their silver content was worth less than their face value.[6] But the 1853 Act left the silver dollar on the coinage list at the old weight, and although it was a monetary unit carrying full legal-tender powers, it was never seen. Silver became the forgotten standard.

Forgotten, however, only a short time; a decade later silver was about to come back. Early in the fall of 1865, a mining inspector named J. L. Ringwalt headed west by train and horse on a special mission for James Pollock, the Director of the United States Mint at Philadelphia. Ringwalt was to inspect and report on operations at the Denver branch of the Mint as well as to survey mining conditions in the Rocky Mountain region. In a long letter to Pollock sent from Denver on October 17, 1865, Ringwalt warned the Mint Director that the Denver branch would probably need some new equipment before long, because new silver mines discovered in the Argentine and Snake River districts "will soon be rendered productive, and . . . methods for saving large amounts of silver and copper from ores which have heretofore been treated exclusively for gold will be adopted." [7]

New silver strikes, and new technology to deal with them: these would become frequent and disturbing events in the monetary world for the next several years. Ringwalt's letter was nothing less than an early indicator that long-established trends in bullion supplies were about to be reversed.

Secretary of the Treasury Hugh McCulloch kept a vigilant eye on mining developments. Following Ringwalt's report the Secretary asked Congress to appropriate $10,000 for further in-

6. They were further debased in 1965, when the Treasury created the "sandwich" dimes and quarters, for the very same reason.
7. U.S. National Archives, Record Group 104 (Records of the U.S. Mint at Philadelphia), Letters to the Secretary of the Treasury. (Hereinafter referred to as NA, RG 104, to Sec. Treas.)

vestigations. This Congress did on July 28, 1866, and on the same day McCulloch appointed James W. Taylor and J. Ross Browne as "special commissioners" to go to different parts of the American West and make detailed surveys of mining conditions. Taylor's assignment was mainly to the region east of the Rockies, and his report, submitted the following February, was only mildly encouraging about new discoveries.

But Browne's report, sent to McCulloch by steamer from San Francisco late in November of 1866, was something else again. Browne had visited California and Nevada, and his conclusion was that "The chief gold mines of California, high as their product is, are small affairs when compared with the vast works of the chief silver companies of Nevada." California gold production was decreasing, as it had for thirteen years, and there was no substantial prospect of new strikes, or of new technological devices to exploit less tractable ores. But Nevada silver production had an excellent future. Mining stock had jumped upward in 1865 and 1866 in the Comstock area, where in 1852 there had been a gold strike involving ore that was up to fifty-percent silver, and where in 1859 miners struck silver ore with the tremendous assay of three thousand dollars to the ton. Browne was a trustworthy observer, and his report was anything but a "boomer" document. Frank and cautious at every point, the report warned that if the Comstock were ever to yield more than a small fraction of its wealth, a tunnel would be needed to "drain the vein to a depth of 2,000 feet." But such a tunnel was already under way—the "Sutro Tunnel Project"—and "Of the continuation of the mining there could be no reason to doubt."

What would it yield? Browne quoted at some length from an 1866 report on the Comstock made by Ferdinand Baron Richtofen, Dr. Phil., a mining scientist. Richtofen had concluded that the Comstock was unlike Hungarian and like Mexican lodes in that it would widen, not narrow, as it deepened. Most important, "the continuity of the ore-bearing character of the Comstock lode in depth must, notwithstanding local interruptions, be assumed as a fact of equal certainty with the continuity of the vein itself"; and "it may positively be assumed that the ores in the Comstock lode will retain their character of true silver ores to indefinite depth." This satisfied Browne, and it satisfied the Mint Director and the Secretary of the Treasury, whose official reports that year noted no serious obstacle to a major increase in available silver except technological ones, which were being overcome by the Sutro Tunnel and new refining techniques using sulfuric acid. The Mint Director further stated that "the most formidable difficulty"—getting the bullion out of Nevada and to the Mint and open markets—"is that which is gradually to be obviated by the introduction of railroad travel and transportation." As it happened, the transcontinental railroad was well under way and would be completed in a little more than two years. In 1867 McCulloch sent Browne on another investigatory trek to the West, and Browne confirmed the trends he had found earlier. The Treasury could look forward, whether it liked it or not, to increases in American silver production and available silver bullion.[8]

What would happen if silver became more plentiful, if it actually slipped in market price to something like the one-to-sixteen ratio? Quite a few disturbing things. Just as gold had driven silver out of circulation years earlier, silver would then drive gold out of circulation; the famous "Gresham's Law," that "bad money drives out good money," would operate again. There would be inconvenience and nervousness among the public. People would have to accustom themselves to silver rather than the gold they knew. They would be forced to use a much more cumbersome metal in trade. Moreover, any contracts or debts that specified payment in gold would be harder to pay; people would have to try to buy gold with silver, and would probably have to pay a premium just as they were doing when they bought gold with greenbacks. Any contracts that specified payment in "coin"—and the United States bonded debt, as refunded after 1870, specified exactly this—would be legally payable in silver rather than in the gold that bondholders gen-

8. Browne's report is U. S. House Executive Document 29, 39 Cong. 2 Sess. (quotes are from pp. 34–35); Treasury and Mint reports are House Executive Document 2, 39 Cong. 2 Sess. (quote from p. 236), and House Executive Document 2, 40 Cong. 2 Sess.

erally had been expecting. This would mean that confidence in the national credit would be shaken, and future bond flotations would be doubly difficult; moreover, from the sheer moral standpoint of full repayment of creditors, redemption of debts in silver might well be construed as somewhat shady. If gold were really driven out of circulation, the whole American economy, public and private, would be at a tremendous disadvantage internationally because neither existing nor future contracts could be fulfilled with any foreign creditor—bond buyer, merchant, shipper, manufacturer, or whatever—who demanded payment in gold. This would include practically everyone in England, the world's financial and trading center, and others elsewhere—collectively, the bulk of the parties with whom the United States dealt in world economic affairs.

On the other hand, there were arguments that silver would not be all that monstrous. If it really became plentiful, either as a prevailing currency or combined with greenbacks, those sections and groups that were short of currency, and short of money in any form, would have more to do with; it would be a monetary shot in the arm for them. Furthermore, if one believed that the real future of United States economic life, domestically and in world trade, lay not in its ability to borrow but in its ability to produce and sell goods, then more abundant money at home was an advantage, not a fault. Produce and distribute successfully, so this argument went, and a favorable monetary position would follow naturally. Even in the short run, there was no good reason to fear silver: the United States was legally on a bimetallic standard; the Civil War bond acts, when they specified coin payment at all, admitted silver on equal terms with gold; even the refunding act of 1870 did the same. If creditors expected gold and objected to silver, their expectations and objections were unreasonable.

Silver production did increase greatly in the late sixties and early seventies, just as Browne and others had predicted, and railroad and mining technology enabled the new silver to move into world markets very quickly. The Comstock experienced major strikes in 1866 and 1870, a number of smaller strikes through the whole period, and in 1873 the greatest bonanza of all, Mackay and Fair's discovery of a silver lode that turned out to be worth more than $250-million—well over fifty percent of the value, incidentally, of the whole outstanding greenback issue of the United States.[9]

The curve of silver bullion being brought to the Mint for coinage under the existing bimetallic laws shot up swiftly in the early seventies; the silver presented in 1872 alone was greater than the combined amount presented in the first several decades of American history. Demonetization in early 1873 stopped this process.

But the arguments against silver, the disastrous consequences that would follow from its replacing gold, were the ones that influenced American policy-makers through the postwar years. The pro-silver position did not prevail until several years after Congress had demonetized silver and placed the United States on the single standard of gold.

9. Rodman W. Paul, *Mining Frontiers of the Far West, 1848–1880* (New York: Holt, Rinehart and Winston, 1963), especially pp. 108–09.

3

Other People's
Money Questions

〰〰〰〰〰〰〰〰〰〰〰〰〰〰〰〰〰〰〰〰〰〰〰〰〰

THE AMERICAN money question had international reper-
cussions—in the international bond market, in net trade and
payments balances, and in the attitude of foreign parties to
someone else's monetary standard. Was there an economic context or business cycle that was world-wide and affected others
and America too? Were events occurring abroad that had long-
term if unforeseen monetary effects, as the Civil War had
domestically?

Few things under the sun are less new than monetary and
currency problems. During the present decade, talk has been
frequent and agitated about looming international liquidity
crises, runs on the dollar and the pound sterling, the obsoles-
cence of the Bretton Woods arrangements of World War II and
the need for a new international reserve unit. Severe economic
disorder in the early 1930's forced Britain and the United
States, among other countries, off the gold standard domestically and, to a considerable extent, in foreign transactions. The
fall of the gold standard seemed to many the fall of civilization,
as it had seemed the talisman of civilization to the men of the
sixties and seventies. Through the 1920's, international financial
diplomats worked manfully to maintain the gold standard, apparently so universally triumphant before 1914, despite the
profound dislocations wrought by World War I. (A completely
satisfactory system of international payments, in fact, has even
yet to be devised.) The only really certain lessons of the post-
1914 era seem to be negative: what happens to the economy of

one major country is bound to affect the others monetarily; gold is very hard to get away from in international payments systems; but gold alone cannot do the job.

Only one of these lessons was at all clear during the period from the 1860's to World War I: that the major countries of the world were becoming increasingly interrelated economically and monetarily. In recent centuries the world's monetary metals (except for minor coins) had generally come to be gold and/or silver. By the mid-nineteenth century, Great Britain and a handful of other countries used gold alone as a standard (gold monometallism). Silver was the standard in the Germanies and Austria, in Scandinavia, Russia, much of Latin America, and in India, China, and Japan. Bimetallism, the double standard of gold and silver fixed legally in a ratio of one unit of gold to somewhere between fifteen or sixteen units of silver—the ratio varied from country to country—prevailed in France and most of Latin Europe, the United States, and a few other places. This potentially chaotic diversity of monetary standards worked reasonably well as long as there were no massive changes in the relative world supplies of refined gold and silver, and as long as the economies (and economic crises) of various countries were relatively independent.

But both of these conditions changed from the middle of the nineteenth century onward. Great changes in bullion stocks did occur, and vast advances in the technologies of production, transportation, and communication together with all of the factors connected with what William H. McNeill has dubbed "the Western Explosion", welded the economies of the world more and more into a world economy.[1] With the progressive establishment of a world economy came a much increased sensitivity of one part of the world to economic and monetary changes in other parts, and an increasing tendency of nations to adopt the same monetary standard, and it was gold that was winning, not losing. Thus the period from the third quarter of the nineteenth century to World War I was the period of the

1. William H. McNeill, *The Rise of the West: A History of the Human Community* (Chicago and London: University of Chicago Press, 1963), pp. 730ff.

triumphant spread of the gold standard. Japan, India, and Russia adopted it at or just before the turn of the century; France and her monetary allies, more in the forefront of world economic integration, effectively joined the gold nations in the mid-seventies; the United States demonetized silver in 1873; and the German Empire declared for gold within months after its creation in 1871. England, the first nation to experience the Industrial Revolution, was also the first major nation to adopt the single gold standard, which she did in Lord Liverpool's Coinage Act of 1816, just after the close of the Napoleonic Wars.

Viewed in sweeping terms, the increasing interdependence of the world's industrializing countries and the parallel triumph of the gold standard take on a neat simplicity and even an aura of inevitability. But, as often happens in history, a closer look shows even so seemingly clear-cut a trend as the spread of gold in the half-century before World War I to have been the product of a myriad of forces, whose arrangement into a long-term pattern was almost wholly unintended, unforeseen, and irregular. The whole process was a surprising sum-total of separate series of events in certain countries.

Nowhere was the process more beset by the turns of history than in France. From the day in 1852 when President Louis-Napoleon Bonaparte proclaimed himself Napoleon III, Emperor of the French, he strove to consolidate France's leadership on the Continent. The quest for progress and *gloire* was undertaken along every path Napoleon and his ministers could find —support for Italian unification, fostering of railroad and other economic development at home, the rebuilding of Paris, and (most importantly for this story) the attempt to make the franc the basic monetary unit of Europe, outstripping the pound sterling as the leading currency in world trade.

By pursuing so many paths to *gloire* the Emperor and his cohorts seemed to be running off wildly in all directions at once. But the goal of French monetary hegemony was by no means silly or quixotic: France had a strong economy, large resources, and efficient financial machinery. She also had a more logical currency system than any other country's. The franc was not only a decimal currency, but was based firmly, the French believed, on immutable scientific fact because the size and weight of the silver franc were integral multiples of the gram and the meter, and the meter in turn was a decimal fraction of the "eternal" circumference of the earth itself. The measurement turned out to be not quite eternal, because of a slight error in calculation, as some English astronomers demonstrated with not quite repressed glee. But the French shrugged aside that nagging fact, and maintained their belief that logic, reason, and science were on their side. That being so, progress and *gloire* could not be far away.

The vehicle for making the franc the basic European currency was a peculiar and nearly forgotten movement, widespread in the 1850's and '60's, to unify the world's standards of weights and measures. The mid-Victorian Age was intoxicated with science, reason, and progress; the breaking down of "artificial" barriers between peoples, such as national boundaries or "outmoded and irrational" customs, seemed within reach. To many men of that day, not only in France but all over the Western world, the differences in standards of weights and measures—and money—among nations was a situation unworthy of modern civilization. Such differences inhibited trade, inconvenienced travellers, and emphasized national idiosyncrasies. Hence it was logical to do away with the differences. International societies sprang up after 1850 dedicated to unifying standards of weights and measures, and because so many thought it essential for money to consist of precious metals, things that could be weighed and measured, coinage quickly became a third object of international unification. Since the French had the most logical system of weights and measures, and since the franc was tied to it, the French could easily play on the international standards unification movement to achieve their own purpose of national *gloire*.

At an International Statistical Conference at Paris in 1855, delegates of several nations agreed that coinage unification ought to be tied to weights and measures unification. At another such Conference, held in Berlin in 1863, the American delegate, Samuel Bulkley Ruggles of New York, proposed that the best way to unify the world's coinages was for the Americans to reduce slightly the gold content of the dollar, and for the British to reduce the gold pound sterling (the "sovereign") by a little less; this would have made five dollars and the pound exactly equivalent to twenty-five gold French francs. Nothing came of the proposal, but the episode showed the French that they could probably count on American support—on the condition that the new international unit be made of gold.

Though France was a bimetallic nation, her gold mono-metallists held the upper hand, if shakily, for the next few years. In 1865 the French succeeded in getting Belgium, Italy, and Switzerland to agree to a treaty unifying the coinages of the four countries. Greece, Rumania, and the Papal States agreed to this so-called "Latin Monetary Union" within the next sixteen months. The first great step had been taken toward international coinage unification, using the franc as the base.

In 1867 the French tried to broaden the Latin Monetary Union at an International Monetary Conference held in conjunction with the Paris Exposition of that year. Aided by the lack of sympathy for bimetallism that existed among her Latin partners, and aided even more by the fierce gold monometallism of certain Americans involved in the Conference,[2] the French got the delegates to agree that any new international coin would be based on the franc—and the gold franc, not the silver one. The American delegate, again Mr. Ruggles of New York, later called the single gold standard "the cardinal, if not the all-important feature of the plan proposed by the Conference."

The declaration of the 1867 Conference was undoubtedly the greatest single boost that universal gold monometallism had ever had. Its effects, however, were to be greater in other countries than in France herself. France was still legally bimetallic, and for two years after the Conference of 1867, bimetallists regained enough control of policy-making machinery to prevent a change to gold. Before the monometallists could regain the offensive, the Second Empire itself crumbled under Prussian guns. France, like the United States nine years earlier,

2. For the full tale see below, chapter 5.

had to abandon specie payments altogether under the stress of war. After the Prussian nightmare and its sequel, the Paris Communard revolt, stopped in 1871, France was liable for an indemnity to the new German Reich of several billion gold francs, and her economic and financial system had to be rebuilt. The times were hardly auspicious for a shift to gold monometallism. It was not until half a decade later, in an entirely different set of circumstances, that the money question re-emerged. Thus France had been a prime mover in the trend toward the universal gold standard, for peculiar nationalistic reasons, but in the end was completely unable to adopt gold monometallism herself.

For Prussia, France's opponent, the story was almost exactly the reverse. Bismarck was no less willing than Napoleon III had been to use the monetary standard and currency and coinage systems as an instrument of diplomacy and politics. But Bismarck began with different working conditions and a different object in mind. In the 1860's the more than two dozen German states were on the single standard of silver, as they had been traditionally. Bismarck's overriding objective was to unify these states into a German Empire under Prussian leadership, with Austria excluded. The Prussian Chancellor used blood and iron to do this, as is well known. But, less dramatically, he also used gold.

Though the sixties, as Bismarck's blood-and-iron policy brought more and more of the Germanies under Prussian hegemony, periodic meetings of economists and businessmen brought the area closer and closer to the gold standard. Leaders of these conferences and leaders of the Prussian Government reinforced each other in their gold-monometallist faith, and then proselytized others. The most successful and dramatic such occasion was the 1868 meeting at Berlin of the *Deutsche Handelstag,* a kind of national association of businessmen. Dr. Adolph Soetbeer, a leading economist very much in tune with Prussian policy, piloted through the Handelstag a resolution favoring the adoption of the single gold standard according to the plan of the Paris Conference of 1867. A further resolution that "directed special notice" to the gold five-franc coin as a basic unit, apparently introduced to placate the major South German states (Bavaria, Baden, Württemburg), which had a large French trade, passed by the thinnest of margins. The Germans were willing to shift to the gold standard, but not in the French style. Bismarck must have been delighted.[3]

Within the next two years the South German states swung into the Prussian orbit after France declared war in 1870. The Prussians' sudden and irreversible victory set the stage for the creation of the German Reich: Prussia's King became Germany's Kaiser. It also set the stage for the adoption of the gold standard in Germany. With the South German states part of the Reich, and with France pledged by the peace treaty to pay Germany a war indemnity of five billion francs in gold, Bismarck finally had motive, opportunity, and wherewithal. Laws of the Empire in 1871 and 1873 adopted gold as the standard, and the gold mark as the coin of the realm; silver coins could be withdrawn at the discretion of the Imperial Chancellor (Bismarck). The new mark was different in weight and size from the franc, the pound, or the dollar: so much for international coinage unification. But gold served the purposes of *national* unification by differentiating German money from Austrian, or French, or any other kind. Bismarck, like Napoleon III, had used the monetary standard as an instrument of policy, but (as in other matters) with signally greater success. Later in the seventies the Chancellor would be quick to apostasize from the monometallist faith when events demanded it. But gold had won a great victory, perhaps its greatest; what was viewed as a "liberal" reform had triumphed for reasons of state.

Britain scarcely had a controversial "money question" during this period. She not only escaped the upheaval of the Franco-Prussian War, but also underwent no struggle to estab-

3. *Verhandlungen des Vierten Deutschen Handelstages zu Berlin vom 20 bis 23. Oktober 1868* (Berlin: Verlag von Stilke & von Muyden, 1868), p. 28. Soetbeer's arguments for his proposals are worth noting, because they indicate what he, the most influential economist in Germany, thought of silver in 1868. Amid appeals to nationalism and cupidity, he warned that silver prices were falling, and that the fall would get worse: a decline in India's demand for silver, and increases in production in Nevada and elsewhere, as well as other developments, proved this, he said.

lish gold, since gold had been the British standard for half a century. The gold standard, in fact, seemed to British economic commentators one of the fundamental reasons for their country's manufacturing and trading pre-eminence. Gold was holy writ. Her Majesty's Government did send delegates to international monetary conferences, but mainly, so it seems, to keep an eye on France. A Royal Commission which met in 1868 to discuss the international coinage unification plan of the Paris Conference recommended extreme skepticism concerning any monetary changes whatever, except the extension of Britain's gold standard to other countries.[4] Despite support for the Paris plan from several worthies, including Gladstone's Chancellor of the Exchequer, Robert Lowe, a lively controversy in Parliament and the City of London in 1869 produced nothing but a reaffirmation of established policy. Britain made a new coinage law in 1870, but made no change in the weight or fineness of the sovereign, kept the gold standard intact, and in fact made gold easier and silver harder to coin. The confidence of official and commercial Britain in gold monometallism, and in the benefits it held in store for the world if it were adopted universally, was unshakeable. So it remained until the mid-seventies.

Viewed against the trend toward the gold standard, and away from silver monometallism or gold-silver bimetallism, international standards and coinage unification on the metric system or the franc basis were sideshows. Another point is that the spread of gold, though it was touted as a liberal, progressive reform, was undertaken in each country for specific nationalistic reasons. As gold monometallism spread, it did so to the satisfaction of the British, the triumph of the Prussians, and the ultimate discomfiture of the French.

The policies of the major European nations had the long-term effect of making the demand for gold greater and the demand for silver less. Gold was increasing, silver decreasing, in monetary popularity. These trends seemed logical and liberal, but what would happen, in an increasingly interdependent economic

4. British Parliamentary Papers, xxvii, "Report of the Royal Commission on International Coinage" (1867–68), p. xviii.

world, if gold became too scarce, or silver too plentiful, or if depression struck?

The four great capitalist countries—America, Britain, France, and Germany—may have had their own political aims and problems. Individually they may have been affected deeply by internal events, such as the American Civil War, that affected the others relatively little. But the technological progress they all worshipped was linking them more closely all the time. In particular, the steamship, the railroad, and the international telegraph were sensitizing them more and more to each other's economies and finances. The bond sales of one country depended on the buyers of another. The prices received by grain growers in Iowa or East Prussia depended on each other's production trends and on prices in Liverpool. Producer durables such as steel rails were becoming articles of world competition as the other countries strove to catch Britain in the industrializing process. With gold and silver the only completely acceptable means of international exchange, any serious change in the world's available bullion supply was bound to have effects everywhere.

Both the business cycle and the bullion supply fluctuated severely during this period, and the fluctuations in the four major countries resembled each other closely and rippled through most of the rest of the world as well. Through most of the sixties and until midway into 1873, economic conditions in the major nations ranged from moderately good to prosperous.[5] The early seventies, in particular, saw tremendous railroad investment in the United States and Britain, and corporate investment in general in Germany. Wholesale prices in England and Germany inflated nearly to American levels, which remained fairly constant just then. The French finished paying their huge war indemnity to Germany only two years after the peace treaty was signed, but while Germany's great influx of gold fostered invest-

5. The serious qualifications were the war boom into 1865 and postwar recession in 1866–67 in the U.S.; the Overend, Gurney Panic of 1866 and subsequent year and a half of depression in Britain; depression and panic in France during and just after the Franco-Prussian War; and a brief recession in Germany in 1867 after the Seven Weeks' War with Austria.

ment and speculation there, the corresponding outflow did not retard France's productive expansion or harm her credit. The several-year period just prior to mid-1873 was, at least economically, one of the happier periods of the whole nineteenth century.

Not so the rest of the decade. Financial panics struck Berlin and Vienna in May, 1873, setting off a slide in wholesale prices and a deepening depression that did not really dissipate until late in 1879. The wholesale price index also bent downward abruptly in Britain toward the end of 1873, and continued to fall; British India underwent successively worse famines; and the British depression did not end until American buying turned the curve of business upward late in 1879. France was least hard-hit of the major countries, but even she slipped into depression in 1877 and 1878. In the United States, the failure of the great banking house of Jay Cooke & Co. in September, 1873, set off a financial panic that heralded a five-year depression involving a drop in wholesale prices, lower wages, and much reduced investment, particularly in railroads. The seventies were a depression decade everywhere, conditions varying from country to country only in the severity of their bleakness. France was least troubled, America more than France but less than England and Germany, who were hit hardest. What was happening to all countries was the first and very unpleasant stage in a world-wide deflationary trend that was to last until just before 1900.[6]

The general business pattern of widespread activity in the late sixties, taking off into inflation until mid-1873, was therefore stopped suddenly by panics and price downturns that led into more-or-less severe depressions until the very close of the seventies. These upheavals were paralleled by different but closely related fluctuations in the world's bullion stocks.

6. Warren M. Persons *et al.,* "Business and Financial Conditions Following the Civil War in the United States," *Review of Economic Statistics,* Supplement, Preliminary Volume II (1920), 9–17; Willard L. Thorp, *Business Annals* (New York: National Bureau of Economic Research, Inc., 1926), pp. 79*ff.*; J. T. W. Newbold, "The Beginnings of the World Crisis, 1873–96," *Economic History* ("A Supplement to the *Economic Journal*"), II (1932), 425–41.

The discovery of gold in California and Australia in the late 1840's had been the most remarkable mining event since the Spanish opened and exploited New World precious-metals sources in the sixteenth century. Gold flowed into circulation in such quantity that it became significantly less valuable relative to silver than legislative ratios said it was. In countries on a bimetallic standard, silver coins disappeared from circulation either to be hoarded or melted down and sold at a profit for gold. By the mid-fifties the new gold supplies seemed so threatening to established ratios that the prominent French monetary theorist Michel Chevalier urged that gold be demonetized, and many people thought the suggestion a good one. But the influx of new gold slackened at about that time, and it was becoming clear that the new gold stocks were not inflating prices in anything like the direct ratio that many had feared it would. By the sixties, gold was still overvalued and silver was still out of circulation in most countries, except for coins purposely debased to such a level that there was no profit in melting them down. It was the customary standard in the United States, the legal standard in Britain, and the prospective standard in France and the Germanies.

Silver, however, was about to come back.

The silver strikes in the United States of the sixties reverberated in Europe. Professor William Stanley Jevons stated in the London *Economist* in May, 1867, that he believed the long-term decline in the price of gold relative to silver had ended (in fact, silver prices had started slipping in 1859). Adolph Soetbeer used his belief in a drop in silver prices as an argument for gold monometallism at the *Deutsche Handelstag* at Berlin in 1868.[7] Some of the delegates to the 1867 Paris monetary conference had already said the same thing. In short, policymakers and monetary experts in the leading countries, the people whose professional business it was to know, were expecting by 1867 or even earlier that silver production would shortly run so substantially ahead of gold production that the long-time undervaluation of silver would cease, and silver would almost

7. Jevons' article was reprinted in the *Bankers' Magazine,* (New York, July 1869), pp. 6–11; for Soetbeer see above, p. 45, *n*3.

undoubtedly return to circulation at the European ratio of one to fifteen-and-a-half, and quite possibly even at the American ratio of one to sixteen. There was a distinct chance that the silver price would drop far enough to drive gold from circulation.

Faced with a flood of new silver, governments already favorably disposed toward the gold standard had yet another reason for demonetizing the white metal. Each move toward demonetization, however, pushed silver prices farther down and made silver even less attractive to those who still held it. Of these moves, the German switch in 1871 and 1873 from silver to gold monometallism was the chief; it threw millions of dollars' worth of silver thalers in silver stocks on a market already declining from increased production, while the concomitant introduction of the new Imperial gold coinage put a heavy added demand on a world gold supply that was remaining relatively stable. The Germans had a sure source of gold, at least within broad limits, in the French war indemnity, but for everyone else the action of the Reich was a major depressant of silver and appreciator of gold.

The final blow to any semblance of stability in silver prices came in 1874 and 1875 from the other side of the world. India, with its vast population and, like other major Asian countries, a silver standard, had always been counted on to soak up large amounts of silver. Rather abruptly, it stopped doing so. European-financed railroad building ground to a halt after the beginning of the world-wide depression in 1873, and successive famines further reduced Indian silver demand as India had less and less to sell on world markets.

Silver, so scarce in the early sixties, thus came into astonishing superabundance by the mid-seventies. The huge increase in supply from Nevada and elsewhere, coupled with the technology needed to bring it very quickly to market, occurred at the very time that demand plummeted because of the effective moratorium on the Indian market and the demonetizations in Germany, several of her northern economic satellites, and the United States. And almost every one of these factors increasing the supply and lowering the demand for silver involved a corresponding increase in the demand for gold.

While all this was happening, of course, the major nations were plunging almost simultaneously into depression, which brought demands in all four of the major countries for increases in the supply of money. As silver fell to a low point in 1876, the major governments did what they could to stabilize silver prices and to return silver, at least to some limited extent, to circulation. The Bismarck Government put aside its long-announced plans to retire the pre-imperial silver coinages of the German states; the French Republican Government of Léon Say had to suspend silver coinage but refused to abolish the bimetallic standard; the Americans restored some silver coinage in 1878; and even the British, under heavy pressure from people and companies with Indian interests, retreated from their earlier position that gold was best for everybody and accepted bimetallism within the Empire.

The major nations were experiencing *en masse* what the British had undergone on a more local scale since their conversion to the gold standard in 1816: when economic conditions were good, the gold basis seemed to work splendidly; when depression hit, gold proved very constricting. The political and diplomatic movement toward the universal gold standard, apparently so successful during prosperity, halted and began to reverse when depression began in 1873. The pattern seems clear today. But it was not at all clear at the time, and policy-makers in the United States and other major countries continued to regard gold monometallism as the natural and normal state of affairs.

There was no inevitability about the onward march of the gold standard in political or economic terms alone. What made it so apparently irresistible was that the ideology and rhetoric of gold monometallism had become an *idée fixe* among those people, in Washington and other capitals, who were in a position to affect the course of legislation. Politically desirable and economically feasible it may have been, but if conviction had been lacking in the minds of powerful men that gold monometallism was ideologically and morally the only proper standard, gold could not have spread as it did.

4

Monetary Ideology: The Wars of the Godly

~~~~~~

THE DEVELOPMENT of the money question during Reconstruction is an interesting problem in historical motivation, because it was at once naively simple and darkly mystifying. The financial straits in which America found herself, or at least in which her policy-makers found her, at the close of the Civil War, obviously demanded solution. The *realpolitischen* schemes of Napoleon III, Bismarck, and the British are understandable enough. The business cycle, bouncier in those days than it has been of late, was also a shaper of events. But explanation cannot stop there. Even with these factors clarified, it is still puzzling why bullion seemed so crucial and why the money question became so central.

The best solution to the puzzle lies in "intellectual" history —a too-dignified name, perhaps, for what in this case was a curious grab-bag of notions, slogans, theories, and verbally expressed moral desires. Monetary legislation was to a very large extent moral wish-fulfillment. To understand it, one not only has to know something of the politics and economics of the time, but also its wish-systems.

In ideology as in politics and economics, the period divides roughly into a time of tranquillity up to 1874, and a time of troubles afterward. The prevailing outlook in the earlier years was liberal in the *laisser-faire* Cobdenite sense, utilitarian in the tradition of Bentham and Mill, mechanistic in the tradition of Newtonian physics and classical economics. These presuppositions led most people, in England and Europe as well as in the United States, to believe in bullion as the natural basis of money, and in money as the ultimate reality in the economic system. Bullion could be touched, held, and squeezed. It had, in a ubiquitous phrase of the time, "intrinsic value"; [1] beyond it one could not go in a search for a fixed point in the economic universe; and economic value was often translated explicitly into scientific and moral value. The majority of bullionists were gold monometallists in all of the major countries except France, where bullionists divided fairly evenly into gold monometallists and gold-silver bimetallists, and a common metaphor identified gold as the sun around which the economic universe revolved, with silver as the moon, a glowing satellite. The metaphor was as rickety in economics as it was in astronomy, but it stated the "natural" order of things well enough for many people.

In many historical instances the connection between theoretical ideas and policy, or between theoreticians and policy-makers, is vague. In this case, however, theorists, publicists, and policy-makers used almost identical phraseology, were often personally acquainted and in correspondence, and sometimes even combined their various roles in a single career. Theorists and policy-makers alike felt themselves in the vanguard of civilization and reform; the gold monometallists in particular were frequently exponents of free trade and other liberal policies. There was a prevailing orthodoxy, a conventional wisdom, that crossed the Atlantic and the boundaries of nations. It also crossed the line that we customarily draw between ideologues and activists—between people who formulate and propagate ideas, and people who formulate and execute legislation. Richard Cobden, the great English free-trader, was the translator into English of the work of the leading French monometallist, Michel Chevalier, and Cobden and Chevalier in 1860 were the negotiators for their governments of a very liberal and very progressive Anglo-French treaty of free trade. Samuel Hooper of Massachusetts was not only a merchant magnate but the author of an influential pair of books on banking and currency; he also, as a Congressman, was responsible

---

1. Which actually and dismayingly appeared in a letter to the editor of *The Times* of London as recently as the spring of 1965.

for parts of the Civil War legislation and in 1872 steered the silver demonetization bill through the House of Representatives. Treasury Secretaries McCulloch and Boutwell corresponded not only with bankers and men of affairs but with academic monetary theorists. The membership list of the Cobden Club of London, a clearing-house for liberal reform, was studded with professors and policy-makers from every great capitalist country: Gladstone, Hugh McCulloch, Prince Jerome Napoleon, and von Delbrück (the Imperial German Finance Minister) were among the celebrated members. Though Garibaldi's presence on the list might suggest that not all members were financial experts of the most knowledgeable sort, the conclusion is unavoidable that the financial thinkers and doers of all leading countries met with each other at least occasionally and were known to each other.[2]

Except in one important particular—the split between gold monometallism and gold-silver bimetallism—these luminaries were remarkably agreed on the principles and policies that would make the economic world run smoothly. High church or low church, they all belonged to the same bullionist establishment. They were not particularly original as economic thinkers; they owed heavy debts to Adam Smith, most noticeably in their belief that labor was the source of wealth, and to the Utilitarian political economists, especially Ricardo and J. R. MacCulloch. Free mankind from governmental restraints that have accreted over time, get rid of tariffs and tampering with the money standard, put society in accord with the laws of nature as scientifically discovered by Smith, Ricardo, Jean-Bap-

2. Among the other members were: from the U.S., Amasa Walker, Francis A. Walker, Edward Atkinson, Arthur Latham Perry, David A. Wells, and Horace White, monetary writers, and James A. Garfield, George Bancroft, S. S. Cox, Carl Schurz, and Samuel B. Ruggles among public men; from Britain, Henry Campbell-Bannerman, Charles Dilke, Cliffe Leslie, Thorold Rogers, Lord Acton, Earl Russell, Lionel Nathan Rothschild, Nathaniel Meyer Rothschild, A. J. Mundella, George Göschen; from France, Victor Bonnet, Léon Gambetta, Louis Wolowski, Léon Say; Emile de Laveleye from Belgium, and an assortment of others economically and politically prominent. (From list of members in Cobden Club of London, *Free Trade and the European Treaties of Commerce. . . .* [London, Paris & New York: Cassell Petter & Galpin, 1875], pp. 133–64.)

tiste Say and a few others, and civilization would progress. The Utilitarians believed that societies that carefully followed natural laws could only be harmonious; that social welfare would be the sum of the self-interests of everyone in society; that pursuit of self-interest, as long as it followed natural laws, was therefore moral (in fact the highest social morality). For the monetary theorists and policy-makers of the time, classical-utilitarian political economy was the doctrine; natural law, civilization, progress, reform, science, the liturgical invocations; trust and probity, public and private, the one great preceptive moral value.[3]

How to realize this moral value in practical affairs? Certainly, by protecting the integrity of the public and private credit. Certainly, by maintaining a sound and stable monetary system. Trust and probity would crumble if a man had no assurance of receiving back what he had lent, or repaying what he had borrowed, because the money and currency he had to use were constantly fluctuating. Moral value meant monetary value; sound money was a moral matter.

· "The economical laws of human nature (i.e. the principles of Political Economy)," declared Francis Bowen in his widely used textbook, "through their general effects upon the well-being of society, manifest the contrivance, the wisdom and beneficence, of the Deity, just as clearly as do the marvellous arrangements of the material universe, or the natural means provided for the enforcement of the moral law and the punishment of crime." [4] Gamaliel Bradford, writing at about the same time in the widely read *North American Review,* agreed: ". . . the laws of finance, like those of other sciences, are universal and invariable in their operation; . . however they may be for a time artificially counteracted [by inconvertible paper currency or other government interference], they will

3. For a more detailed statement of this doctrine, see Elie Halévy, *The Growth of Philosophic Radicalism* (trans. Mary Morris; London: Faber & Faber Limited, 1934), p. 478.
4. Francis Bowen, *American Political Economy, including Strictures on the Management of the Currency and the Finances Since 1861* (New York: Charles Scribner's Sons, 1870), p. 21.

ultimately assert themselves; . . . the mills of God, though they may grind slowly, grind exceeding small." [5] This financial Newtonianism, this deistic faith in natural law and in man's discovery of it in modern civilized times, was part of the same faith and frame of mind that other writers have observed in such prominent figures of that day as William Graham Sumner, Charles Francis Adams, Jr., Andrew Carnegie, and E. A. Godkin.[6] Money was central, money obeyed laws, money came from labor; "The profit on capital is Nature's reward for self-denial," quoth Simon Newcomb, a Harvard astronomy professor who was also an extremely rigorous but highly respected financial authority.[7] The age that could tie coinage questions to the metric system and thus, it thought, to the eternal dimensions of the earth, could easily believe economics and finance to possess the same degree of scientific certainty as astrophysics, and give ear to astronomers when they talked of it; Newton, once Master of the Royal Mint, and Copernicus were favorite authorities. Utilitarianism was simply the extension of Newtonian principles into political and moral affairs.[8]

In the light of these certainties, America's problems had obvious solutions. Move toward free trade; avoid labor unions and other agencies that meddle with the natural harmony of individual self-interests; keep to the bullion standard.[9] As Hugh McCulloch said, in the speech that keynoted his administration of the Treasury Department, "By common consent of the nations, gold and silver are the only true measure of value. They are the necessary regulators of trade. I have myself no more doubt that these metals were prepared by the Almighty for this very purpose, than I have that iron and coal were prepared for

    5. *North American Review* (January 1870), p. 209.
    6. Edward C. Kirkland, *Business in the Gilded Age: the Conservative's Balance Sheet* (Madison: University of Wisconsin Press, 1952); Robert G. McCloskey, *American Conservatism in the Age of Enterprise: A Study of William Graham Sumner, Stephen J. Field and Andrew Carnegie* (Cambridge: Harvard University Press, 1951), esp. pp. 170–71.
    7. *North American Review* (July 1870), p. 133.
    8. As Halévy pointed out: Halévy, *op. cit.,* p. 6.
    9. *Bowen, op. cit.,* pp. 114–17; *North American Review* (July 1870), 123–28.

the purposes in which they are being used." [10] Gold was natural, scientific, civilized, progressive, liberal. "Every argument in favor of paper money is a fallacy unworthy of the nineteenth century," snorted Simon Newcomb.[11] "Gold and silver have been recognized for many ages, by the general consent of mankind, as the standard of value . . . they constitute the only real money of commercial nations", Congressman Samuel Hooper affirmed, because they are "comparatively of an unvarying value" and because they "have an intrinsic value, independent of their use for money." [12] Amasa Walker, another respected Yankee authority, spoke for many when he stated that "The true Standard of Value exists in nature, is subject to nature's laws, and recognizes no other. Governments have rightfully nothing to do with it. . . . Of all social wrongs, this interference [greenbacks or debased coins] is one of the greatest. It strikes not only at the material interests of the state, but the morals of the people. It establishes injustice by law, and introduces every species of speculation and fraud." [13]

The bullion basis of money—the view, in fact, that bullion was the only money—was thus a firmly-grounded theorem of "moral science." With its Newtonian, classical-economic, and utilitarian underpinnings, it was a secular religion. The split between gold monometallists and gold-silver bimetallists was consequently akin to a theological dispute. And it was serious. Bimetallic theory was understandably best developed in France —where the two metals actually circulated together. There the leading theorists such as Louis Wolowski prided themselves that "le doute scientifique de Descartes" had gold monometal-

10. *Our National and Financial Future. Address of Hon. Hugh McCulloch . . . at Fort Wayne, Indiana, October 11, 1865* (Fort Wayne: n.p., 1865), pp. 12–13.

11. Newcomb, *A Critical Examination of our Financial Policy during the Southern Rebellion* (New York: D. Appleton and Company, 1865), p. 197.

12. Hooper, *Currency or Money; its Nature and Uses, and the Effects of the Circulation of Bank-Notes for Currency* (Boston: Little, Brown and Company, 1855), pp. 7–8.

13. Amasa Walker, "Governmental Interference with the Standard of Value," speech to American Association for the Promotion of Social Science, reprinted in *Bankers' Magazine* (April 1867), pp. 725, 738.

lism on the run.[14] But bimetallism had few proponents elsewhere. In Britain the leading and nearly the only voice of
bimetallism was a London bullion merchant and financial
writer named Ernest Seyd who argued vehemently that civilization would best be served by the more abundant metallic
money that silver, together with gold, would provide; financial
science as well as tradition demonstrated this.[15] In Germany
bimetallism had almost no advocates, and in the United States
it was virtually unheard of. The usual view was that of the London *Economist,* which considered it a "heresy" and sorrowed
that "Monetary civilization has been much complicated by the
fact that there are two precious metals of which silver, the
bulkier and cheaper, is more suitable to primitive times, and
gold, the rarer and dearer, to civilized times of nicer habits and
with larger transactions.[16] Others pointed out that silver was
the normal standard among the more backward Asians, Slavs,
and Latins, while gold was normal among the Anglo-Saxons
and the few others in the vanguard of civilization and progress.
American writers, for the most part, simply ignored the legal
fact that America was a bimetallic country and that silver had
bullion status. Newcomb, whose main enemy was the greenback, typically remembered that silver did exist but went on to
say that "Gold now is the standard of value in our own as in
every other civilized country," and will continue to be, "in spite
of any thing any Government may do to prevent it." [17] Bullionism, and the gold-monometallic version of it, was the prevailing
orthodoxy in America among theorists and policy-makers alike
before 1873.

The only serious opposition to gold monometallism in pre-
1873 America, or to bullionism in any of the major nations

14. Louis Wolowski, *L'Or et L'Argent* (Paris: Librairie de Guil-
laumin et Cie, 1870), p. 33.

15. Seyd's major book was *Bullion and Foreign Exchanges Theoretically and Practically Considered; Followed by a Defence of the Double
Valuation* . . . (London: Effingham Wilson, 1868); see for example
pp. 657–58.

16. *Economist,* September 15, 1866, 1078, quoted in Henry Parker
Willis, *A History of the Latin Monetary Union* (Chicago: University of
Chicago Press, 1901), p. 73n2.

17. Newcomb, *Critical Examination, op. cit.,* p. 109.

throughout the period, came from a vocal collection of Americans who seriously did believe that a permanent inconvertible paper currency was a good idea. These people were convinced that money was a moral matter, that it was subject to eternal natural laws, especially the law of supply and demand, that civilization and progress demanded proper policy, and that labor was the source of wealth: on all of these grounds there was little to distinguish them from the bullionists. But these "greenbackers" added one important law—that harmonious association was the natural law of human behavior and to perfect it was the object of society. They also made two key interpretations of their principles that the bullionists decidedly did not make: their definition of society was, usually, people organically united into and under national sovereign government; and that since labor was the source of wealth, labor was manifested in production, of which money was nothing more than the accumulated measure. In policy terms, all of this meant that sovereign government, acting on behalf of the people, had the right and duty to increase and distribute money in the interests of production. It meant also that money had in no sense whatever any intrinsically necessary form, such as gold or silver; all it had was a function, which was to measure production. This was the nub of what we can call "the producer philosophy."

Greenbackism thus parted company decisively from bullionism in theory and in policy. If people had bought government bonds with greenbacks during the war, it was robbery of the people to pay them in a currency more valuable, i.e. equivalent to a far larger amount of productive labor, than they had lent. If a greenback currency was needed and available to stimulate trade and nourish production, it was a national disgrace to reduce the amount in circulation. Believing as they did that value rested in production and that money was only a measure of it, they opposed any rate of interest higher than the rate of increase in national productivity per year—what we would call today the increase in rate of the gross national product (G.N.P.). This they figured, by rule of thumb, to be one one-hundredth of a percent per day, which works out to 3.65%

per year. Interest above this rate was unjust, because interest *produces* nothing; labor produces everything. As William Sylvis put it in an article reprinted in 1871 in the *Workingman's Advocate,* the organ of the National Labor Union and the vehicle of leading greenback theorists, the prevailing interest rate was 15% per annum, but the increase in productivity about 3%; the other 12% was thus "a lien upon future labor. It is a mortgage upon the productive industry of the country." [18]

Greenbackers opposed interest rates above the productivity increase not only for private debts but for the federal bonds. If the country is to grow, they said, the kind of industry that ought to be fostered is active industry, not passive; passive industry was the industry that had already been performed and was now accumulated in the form of investment capital. Why should this kind of industry draw interest at rates higher than the reward given to active industry, i.e., productive labor? Active industry, in fact, should receive a slightly higher reward— and in monetary policy this meant a perpetual inflation of a very limited sort. The government, as the people's representative, was the only agency with the right to do this (national banks definitely not included). How to do it? How insure that active labor is rewarded at the same rate as passive? By making government bonds interconvertible with greenbacks. The bonds would pay the holder 3.65% interest, the rate equivalent to productivity increases, if the holder preferred to let his accumulated labor behave passively. On the other hand, if he wished to employ it actively, he could convert it into the non-interest-bearing currency which would bring him, presumably, an equivalent return.

Return, interest, production, and labor as related in such ways make sense if and when people were actually producing something. The greenbackers assumed the existence of a "producing class," which they defined rather broadly, but which, so defined, did fit the major segments of the labor force at that time. The majority of the labor force in 1870 was in agriculture; a great many of the rest were artisans or manufacturers, and

18. *Workingman's Advocate* (May 20, 1871).

the line between the latter two was by no means as clear as it was shortly to become. Greenbackism in its early days drew its strength from two groups who during most of subsequent American history have been thought of as opposites: labor and manufacturers.

Not all manufacturers supported greenbackism; well-established ones, such as New England textile people, were as hard-money as their local theorists. But manufacturers in new, expanding businesses, most especially in iron and steel, identified themselves with farmers and laborers and other producers against the "non-producing few" (which usually meant lenders). The great ideologue of the manufacturing-greenback group was Henry C. Carey of Philadelphia, who in the seventies was closing a long career which probably entitles him to the accolade of America's greatest political economist in the nineteenth century. In Carey's view, man's "greatest need is thàt of ASSOCIATION with his fellow-men," and as matter inexorably is attracted by molecular gravitation, thus also "man tends of necessity to gravitate towards his fellow-man." [19] One of the chief ways in which men associated with each other, of course, was economic. Economic activity was natural and good. To promote economic activity, especially production, was therefore to promote association; and nothing promoted it like money. More money, or abundant money, was morally desirable. As Carey's nephew, Henry Carey Baird, later stated, ". . . when Carey treated money as the instrument of association, he placed it on its true philosophical basis, on a higher plane than any writer who had gone before him." [20]

Hence the Careyite support of the greenback. Like the greenbackism of the National Labor Union, manufacturing greenbackism made the productive function the basis of economics and advocated whatever instruments would further production—especially low interest rates and abundant money. Money had a key role in economic life: to facilitate exchange

19. Carey, *Principles of Social Science* (Philadelphia: J. B. Lippincott & Co., 1883 [first published 1858]), I: pp. 41–42.

20. Henry Carey Baird, *John Sherman: A Critical Examination of his Claims to Statesmanship* (Philadelphia: Henry Carey Baird & Co., 1907), p. 4.

and measure production; but it was not essentially tied to one form, certainly not scarce forms such as gold and silver bullion.

Greenbackism was not an inconsiderable force in the land even before 1873. The National Labor Union, its leaders and its publications, advocated it steadfastly, and important manufacturing groups, most prominently the trade association of iron and steel makers centering in Pennsylvania, were convinced Careyites. Carey himself was in frequent personal contact with manufacturing interests and propounded his soft-money and high-tariff ideas in the *Bulletin* of the American Iron and Steel Association.[21] Greenbackism and tariff protectionism resounded in the halls of Congress, most notably from the oft-open mouth of Representative William D. "Pig-Iron" Kelley, a Philadelphia Republican and Carey disciple. But greenbackism never, at any time, secured anything like the degree and extent of loyalty among Treasury and Congressional leaders that the gold monometallist version of bullionism did, and outside the United States, doctrines of inconvertible paper currency simply had no following at all.

As the seventies wore on, greenbackism paradoxically gained in popular support but grew even less likely to control policy and create legislation. A National Greenback political party succeeded in electing some Congressmen in 1876 and subsequent elections, and it mounted vigorous presidential campaigns in 1876 and 1880. But the group and sectional support for greenbackism changed in such a way as to make it even less likely that greenbackism would ever prevail. Masses of American farmers, who had had almost nothing to say about the money question before 1873, became more and more aroused by it after 1873, and many of them became staunch supporters of the greenback. Labor continued to support it. But the critical development was the apostasy of the manufacturers: though Henry C. Carey and his closest disciples actually made the ultimate commitment of joining the Greenback party, the manufacturing group among whom they apparently had

21. See also the Carey letters in the seventies in the James M. Swank Papers, Historical Society of Pennsylvania. Swank was the executive officer of the Association.

had such influence saw themselves less and less as members of a "producing class" in essential harmony with farmers and laborers, more and more as capitalists, enleagued with bankers, great merchants, and railroad magnates. There are several likely reasons for this. Many of them realized greenbackism was hopeless as specie resumption approached, and then became a fact in 1879. Manufacturing was one sector not deeply affected by the post-1873 depression, and was relatively well off compared to manufacturing in other countries. The unit size of manufacturing enterprises, especially in steel and iron, grew during the seventies, and the total production of the industry expanded exponentially. Perhaps above all, increasingly numerous and more violent disputes with labor shocked and soured manufacturers. Moreover, the greenback ideology shared with bullionism many basic assumptions, such as natural law, a belief in progress, the application of science to human affairs, and of course probity and fairness of exchange as the fundamental economic and moral value. With these many points in common, greenback producerites could become bullionists without too great a wrench, especially since practical events seemed so strongly to demand the shift.

For this and other reasons the ideological configurations on the money question in America moved in a bullionist direction after 1873. This by no means meant, however, that pressure for abundant money ceased too. As the greenback heresy faded, as the high-priests of the heresy, Carey and Alexander Campbell, lost their charisma and many of their followers joined the true church of bullionism, the intramural strife within the bullionist edifice was profoundly intensified. Former greenbackers, who shucked off the policy of paper but by no means the philosophy of producerism, massively reinforced the bimetallist minority, and these re-enthused saints thereupon began to propound a new interpretation of the bullionist dogma called "free silver." The gold monometallists, placed on the defensive, responded with an accomodation variously called "limited bimetallism" or "international bimetallism" which would preserve the substance of the gold standard while insuring silver a permanent place in the firmament. The greenbacker insight that money was definable by its function, not its form, was lost; bullionism, either of the limited-bimetallist or the free-silver kind, became the safe and reactionary doctrine. Over the interpretation of that doctrine the money question was fought for the rest of the century.

This was the ideological context of the money question that gave shape and direction, and itself was shaped and directed, by political and economic events. The overriding fact was the way in which bullionism in one version or another conquered the loyalties of nearly everyone. But the greenbackers were probably closer to being radicals than any other group of the time, and the decline of their doctrines among manufacturers, farmers, and eventually even laborers was another sign of the triumph of capitalism and the absence of radicalism in the West.[22]

Everything discussed so far—the legacies of the American Civil War, the political plans and events of the major Western nations, the business cycle, changes in gold and silver stocks, and the configurations of ideologies and group beliefs—coalesced to affect the development of the money question in America during the late sixties and the seventies. Monetary policy was the product of their interplay. The course of policy-making was as complex as its backdrop. But its end result was clear: first, the demonetization of silver in 1873, and then, in the subsequent time of troubles, silver's partial remonetization in such a way as to leave the gold standard essentially intact.

22. For a fascinating neo-Freudian exploration of the connections between personality, capitalism, and society, see Norman O. Brown, *Life Against Death: The Psychoanalytical Meaning of History* (Middletown, Conn.: Wesleyan University Press, 1959), especially chapter XV, "Filthy Lucre," pp. 234–304.

5

The Crime of '73

TWENTY YEARS after Congress and President Grant made law of the Coinage Act of 1873, when times had turned bad again and the money question had once more gripped the public mind, that Act had taken on the shape of legend. From the West and South came ugly charges. The Coinage Act of 1873 was a Crime of '73, a monumental fraud upon the people, committed by a conspiracy of legislators and financiers. English and European bond-holding interests, to make sure that their investments would be paid in gold, sent Ernest Seyd to America in 1872 with £100,000 to smooth the way of silver demonetization through a venal Congress. The act was passed surreptitiously, said some (notably those from silver states who had been in Congress but had not tried to stop the act), and it had fastened a repressive, deflationary gold standard on the helpless masses in the interests of a corrupt few.

That, in briefest terms, was the agrarian legend of the "Crime of '73." But there was another legend of the 1873 Coinage Act. It grew up in response to the agrarian legend and in defense of those who had created and passed the act. It was the position of Senator Sherman in the 1893 debate on the repeal of the Silver Purchase Act of 1890, and it affirmed the innocence of Sherman, other Congressmen, and Treasury officials of any corruption whatever in 1873. The Act of 1873 was debated often and read frequently in many versions before the Congress over a three-year period prior to its passage; there was nothing surreptitious, everything was open and above-board, about the act, its silver provisions, and its method of passage. Silver was practically unheard of in 1873, had been in disuse as a standard and as a dollar coin for over a generation, and showed no signs of life. The Act of 1873 simply recognized reality and brought the law into logical conformity with it, continuing the debasement of silver that had started in the Act of 1853 with regard to the minor coinage. Silver discoveries in Nevada and the subsequent fall in the price of silver were coincidental and unexpected sequels. This was the later view of most of the participants in the passage of the 1873 Act.

This view has become the "orthodox" legend, because it was taken up by the mass of writers on the subject and continues to be pretty much the standard textbook treatment down to the present day. The silver dollar was "an unknown coin. There was nothing secret in the abolition of the piece. . . . Not one party to the passage of the law of 1873 recognized the significance of the abolition of the legally existing double standard," said Neil Carothers in his respected work which others have followed and which is undoubtedly one of the saner histories of American money and finance.[1]

But neither legend—that of the agrarians or that of the orthodox—comes close to the facts.

The legislative history of the Coinage Act of 1873 is a fascinating example of the complexity of motive forces in human political actions and also of the confusion that can later surround these motives. In their haste to defend or condemn, the legend-creators on both sides twisted essential episodes in the story, left out others, failed to connect the demonetization of silver with political, diplomatic, economic, and intellectual trends, and quite lacked the ability to credit their opponents with any sense of public honor. One would think, for example, that George S. Boutwell's testimony on the matter would be a key piece of evidence in any interpretation. Boutwell was Secretary of the Treasury while the coinage bill was being prepared and when it was passed. He stated unequivocally in his memoirs

1. Neil Carothers, *Fractional Money: A History of the Small Coins and Fractional Paper Currency of the United States* (New York: John Wiley & Sons, Inc., 1930), p. 235.

that he had understood what was happening, that the bill had got rid of the silver standard, and that the silver standard ought to have been got rid of in the best interests of the country. But the orthodox legend ignored Boutwell's statement of his foreknowledge; the agrarian legend ignored Boutwell's affirmation of upright motive. Nor was that the only anomaly.

To begin at the beginning.

The Coinage Act of 1873, which dropped the standard 412½ -grain silver dollar from the list of American coins, was not prepared overnight. The bill that ultimately became the act first began to be drawn up in the Treasury Department in the latter part of 1869 and appeared in both Houses of Congress several times, in committees or on the floor, over the next three years. Before that, in January, 1868, Senator John Sherman introduced a bill to make the gold dollar the sole standard monetary unit of the United States at a weight conforming to twenty-five gold French francs. Before that, in spring of 1867, Sherman and others were instrumental in bringing the Paris International Monetary Conference to declare for universal gold monometallism. And in the months before that, monetary experts in several countries knew that silver was about to make a comeback. Soetbeer in Germany and Jevons in England stated it publicly, and the United States Treasury (then trying to bring about specie resumption by the contraction method) was informed of it particularly by the report of J. Ross Browne.

By late 1866, pressure centers began to form whose confluence within a year would produce a trans-Atlantic storm for gold monometallism. Some of these pressures, such as the pressure accumulating for fifteen years toward international adoption of a decimal metric system of weights and measures, would be metamorphosed without great resistance into something more potent, a pressure for intenational gold coinage. Other pressure centers acted less to raise the velocity of the storm than to create favorable conditions for its spread: for example, gold-monometallic Britain, which stayed clear of diplomatic involvement but was certainly amenable to others adopting her own monetary standard and belief; or Prussia, which was already thinking of a shift to gold to help unify Germany, but which was not yet ready to move.

The really powerful pressures, those that soon gave the storm its thrust, came from within France and the United States. In January, 1866, President Johnson approved a House Resolution allowing official American representation at the International Exposition in Paris which, it will be recalled, was to include a section devoted to coinage, weights, and measures. In May, 1866, at the same time that House and Senate approved a law making metric weights optionally legal, Congress voted money for a special commissioner on coinage for the Paris Exposition. The interconnection of personalities is worth noting: Representative John Kasson of Iowa piloted both bills, the one legalizing metric weights and the one appropriating funds for the coinage commissioner, through the House. John Sherman, as Chairman of the Senate Finance Committee, led both bills through the other house. The outstanding private petition for the metric bill came from the New York State Chamber of Commerce and was drawn up and signed by Samuel Bulkley Ruggles. Ruggles became the coinage commissioner at the Paris Exposition by appointment from Secretary of State William Henry Seward in October. Ruggles had been active on a semi-private basis for over a year, together with other prominent New Yorkers, in preparing the American exhibits and plans for the Exposition. Ruggles was also a sometime business associate of Secretary of the Treasury Hugh McCulloch. Although their recorded discussions about the Exposition, the spread of the metric system, and international coinage unification did not involve silver directly, it is clear that there were official relations among the French Government, the American Secretaries of State and of the Treasury, Congressman Kasson, Senator Sherman, and Ruggles by 1866—and Ruggles had proposed back in 1863, as American delegate to the International Statistical Conference at Berlin, the unification of the dollar, the pound, and the franc on the gold basis.[2]

2. Senate Executive Document 5, 39 Cong. 2 Sess., documents relative to the Paris Exposition, incorporating or referring to (*inter alia*) M. de Geoffroy [Consul of France] to Seward, letter, March 27, 1865, pp. 3–5; N. M. Beckwith [American Consul] to Seward, Paris, July 17, 1866, on unifying the dollar, pound, and franc, pp. 23–24; report of

There is no absolutely clear evidence that at that point the principals were working for international gold coinage unification because they expected imminently a drop in silver and a consequent dislocation of commercial and financial values among the trans-Atlantic countries. It is clear, however, that they were all working toward a universal gold standard, because they believed it civilized, convenient, progressive, in accord with natural law; bimetallism did not make sense to them, at least not to the Americans. It is also clear that Treasury officials, and (if not in 1866 then shortly afterward) Senator Sherman as well, were acquainted with the Browne Report and understood what it could mean.

By the time the Paris Exposition opened, the French Government was in the throes of a battle between the previously dominant bimetallists and the hard-attacking gold monometallists. Ruggles had arrived in Paris in late March, 1867, and from that point the game turned slowly but definitely toward the monometallists. By mid-May they were on the verge of victory. Ruggles had worked closely with Michel Chevalier, the leader of the theoreticians of metric gold monometallism, and M. Esquirou de Parieu of the *Conseil d'Etat*. These monometallist sachems needed to play only one more strong card to swing the French Government decisively their way. Ruggles brought out the ace of trumps.

Senator Sherman tells us in his *Recollections* that he was not able to describe his European trip in 1867 in great detail,

---

French *Corps Législatif* incorporated in Beckwith letter noting possibilities of new silver discoveries and recommending retention of bimetallism for France; Seward to Beckwith, State Department, October 4, 1866, notifying Beckwith of Ruggles' appointment and stating that Ruggles had already been in touch with the French about coinage. Also, *House Journal*, 39 Cong. 1 Sess., p. 66, on H. Res. 141 authorizing appointment of a coinage commissioner; *Congressional Globe*, 39 Cong. 1 Sess., debates of May 17–18, 1866, House and Senate, on the metric bill and H. Res. 141; New York State Chamber of Commerce, *Annual Report* (for 1866–67), (New York: John W. Amerman, Printer, 1867), including report of meeting of May 17, 1866, where Ruggles commented on weights and coinage; McCulloch to Ruggles, Treasury Department, April 25, 1865, in McCulloch Papers, Lilly Library of Indiana University; Resolution of New York State Chamber of Commerce, May 19, 1866, in Sherman Papers, Library of Congress.

for "I have no memoranda in respect to the voyage and preserved no letters about it." He did recall, however, that he sailed from New York on April 10, a good ten days before the Senate adjourned its current session, and visited first Ireland, then England, then Paris. He had, he said, no plan in mind; simply "rest, a change of air and scene, and . . . as one of the attractions of the voyage, a visit to the Exposition at Paris in that year." He was fortunate to have as a travelling companion his old friend, Congressman Kasson.[3]

Among the letters the Senator thought he had not saved (they rest today in the Library of Congress) was one sent him the day before he left New York from Congressman Samuel Hooper of Massachusetts (who had a later role to play in silver demonetization) introducing Sherman to the head of Baring Brothers' bank; others he received in London and Paris from English and American officials and financial people. Still another letter was from Ruggles, dated May 17.

The background, or what we know of it, of Ruggles' letter, indicates Franco-American cooperation at a high level toward universal gold coinage. Secretary of State Seward had written the French chief of mission in Washington back in February, 1867, before Ruggles left for Paris, that he (Seward) and the Secretary of the Treasury certainly agreed with France that coinage unification was a desirable thing. Ruggles and Sherman perhaps knew of this correspondence and no doubt understood the Cabinet officials' views. On May 7, according to Ruggles' later official report, M. Esquirou de Parieu asked him to put in writing Ruggles' now-familiar proposal to unify the gold dollar and five gold francs, on the condition that France would coin a twenty-five-franc piece that would be equivalent to the English gold pound. Ruggles felt that he lacked the authority and declined to do this.[4]

3. Sherman, *Recollections of Forty Years in the House, Senate and Cabinet. An Autobiography.* (Chicago: The Werner Company, 1895), p. 396. It must be pointed out, in fairness, that Sherman's memory was slipping badly when he was writing his memoirs.
4. Senate Executive Document 14, 40 Cong. 2 Sess. (Ruggles' report), p. 14; M. Berthemy to Seward, French Legation at Washington, January 4, 1867, pp. 2–3; Seward to Berthemy, State Department, Febru-

But then Sherman appeared. Ruggles' May 17 letter to Sherman reminded the Senator that delegates of several nations were meeting in connection with the Exposition

to agree, if possible, on a common unit of money, for the use of the civilized world. I perceive that the opinions of the Committee are leaning strongly in favor of adopting as the unit, the existing French five-franc piece of gold. May I ask what, in your opinion, is the probability that the Congress of the United States, at an early period, would agree to reduce the weight and value of our gold dollar, to correspond with the present weight and value of the gold five-franc piece of France, and how far such a change would commend itself to your own judgment?

Ruggles asked for permission to make Sherman's reply known to the delegates.

Sherman replied at once from the Hotel du Jardins des Tuileries, a short way down the Rue de Rivoli from the delegates. Although the idea had been debated so little in Congress that he couldn't really say what would happen, he personally thought it a very fine idea. Quite likely the five-franc piece, already being used by over sixty million people (the Latin Union), should be adopted by others, leaving to each country the decision over the disposal of its "silver and token coinage. If this is done the French will surely abandon the impossible effort of two standards of value. . . . The adoption of a common gold standard will regulate silver coinage of which the United States will naturally supply the greater portion." Although he doubted that the United States would join in the project by international treaty, he certainly gave great encouragement about the prospects of approaching Congress on the matter: "I feel sure that Congress will adopt any practical measure that will secure to the commercial world a uniform standard of value and exchange." [5]

ary 13, 1867; Samuel Hooper to Sherman, April 9, 1867, in Sherman Papers, Library of Congress. For an example of Esquirou de Parieu's gold-monometallist views well before the Conference, see his "La question monétaire en France et à l'Etranger", *Revue Contemporaine,* XLVIII (2d series; December 31, 1865), pp. 712–22.

5. Ruggles to Sherman, Paris, May 17, 1867; Sherman to Ruggles, undated draft in Sherman Papers, Library of Congress; latter corresponds

Sherman had hardly stuck his own or his country's neck out very far. But his position as Chairman of the Senate Finance Committee made his opinion worth a very great deal— enough, in fact, that the French Government about a week later sent invitations to foreign powers to attend a full-scale International Monetary Conference, considerably more grand and decidedly more authoritative for the French monometallists than the discussions already in progress. Secretary Seward immediately notified the French that Ruggles, "who is familiar with the views of this Government," would be the American delegate, and the Conference began meeting in mid-June. Sherman was in Paris for at least part of the Conference, and he, Ruggles, Esquirou de Parieu, Kasson, and American Minister John A. Dix were in contact at that time. Meanwhile, Assistant Secretary of State F. W. Seward cabled Ruggles on June 21 saying that Sherman's very able statement would no doubt be concurred in by the public and by the United States Government.[6]

After a Franco-American front had been so solidly established, it was no surprise—though it still took some clever gavel-wielding by Esquirou de Parieu—that the International Monetary Conference decided in favor of the gold five-dollar —pound-sterling—twenty-five-franc international unit, and affirmed that "It is very desirable that the system of two different monetary standards should be abolished wherever it still exists." Ruggles later called the declaration for universal gold monometallism "the cardinal feature" of the Conference's agreements. Many years later, Sherman defended the Conference by pointing out that in 1867 silver was worth more than the American one-to-sixteen ratio, or even the European one-to-fifteen-and-a-half ratio: "No suggestion was made or enter-

---

to printed version dated May 18, 1867, in Senate Executive Document 14, 40 Cong. 2 Sess., pp. 107–08.

6. Senate Executive Document 14, 40 Cong. 2 Sess., Berthemy to Seward, French Legation in Washington, May 27, 1867, p. 5; Seward to Berthemy, State Department, May 29, 1867, p. 6; F. W. Seward to Ruggles, State Department, June 21, 1867. Also, Ruggles to Sherman, Paris, June 12; same to same, Paris, June 20; Dix to Sherman, Paris, June 26; LeGrand Lockwood to Sherman, Paris, June 30, all in Sherman Papers, Library of Congress.

tained to disturb the circulation of silver. The only object sought was to secure some common coin by which other coins could be easily measured. . . . It was perfectly understood that, while silver was the chief coin in domestic exchanges in every country, it was not convenient for foreign commerce, owing to its bulk. . . . It is apparent that the chief cause of the fall of the market value of silver is its increased production. . . . The law of supply and demand regulates value. It is the 'higher law' more potent than acts of Congress." [7] Of this act of faith in liberal economics and the status quo, one can only think that Sherman's sincerity was as great as his memory was faulty.

For various reasons connected with European great-power diplomacy, most of the participants in the Paris Conference of 1867 proceeded very little farther along the road to international coinage unification. The British, always suspicious of French designs for *gloire,* turned the matter over to a Royal Commission; the Germans, as Soetbeer bluntly put it one time in 1868, "must go our own way"; even in France the bimetallists began to regain some control over policy-making. But in the United States, at least for another full year, the plan of the Conference and the gold monometallism that went with it maintained the loyalties and energies of Sherman, Ruggles, Seward, McCulloch, and certain others.

Seward and Berthemy continued their correspondence through August and September. On September 30, 1867, the Secretary of State was able to forward the Frenchman a letter he had received from Secretary McCulloch, declaring the Treasury chief's "cordial concurrence" in the plan of the Paris Conference, particularly the gold standard aspect of it, and stating that he planned to recommend it to Congress at the forthcoming session. By December, Sherman and McCulloch had in hand a rough draft of a bill embodying the Conference proposals and fundamentally changing the coinage of the United States.

At this point, McCulloch called for expert opinion on the man he had recently made Director of the Mint at Philadelphia,

7. Sherman, *Recollections, op. cit.,* p. 412.

Dr. Henry R. Linderman. Writing to Linderman on December 23, McCulloch told him that Senator Sherman was examining the proposed bill for coinage unification and wanted to talk to Linderman about it. Linderman was already quite familiar with the Mint operation, with coinage and currency affairs in the leading countries, and in fact with gold and silver mining conditions in the American West. But this was apparently the first time he had been brought directly into the diplomatic and legislative process: McCulloch presumed Linderman had seen Ruggles' report on the Paris Conference, but sent him a copy anyway, "which will give you a general idea of what is desired to be accomplished. The bill to be prepared will regulate the size and weight of our future gold coinage with a view to unification." A few days later McCulloch wrote to Linderman again, making final the arrangements for the Secretary and Senator Sherman to meet Linderman and another Mint official on December 29.[8]

Senate Bill 217, "in relation to the coinage of gold and silver," which Sherman introduced and had referred to the Finance Committee a week later on January 6, 1868, was thus the immediate brainchild of McCulloch, Sherman, and Linderman. It had two important provisions. First, it would reduce the gold content of the gold dollar by 3.5 percent, which would make the gold dollar exactly "equiponderant" to the French gold five-franc coin; this, together with a hoped-for smaller reduction by the English of the gold in the sovereign would make the coins of the three nations equivalent. This, of course, had been Ruggles' plan for years (at least since the Berlin Conference of 1863), and it was the recommendation of the International Monetary Conference of 1867. Second, the bill would drop the silver coins of one dollar, five cents, and three

8. Seward to Berthemy, State Department, September 30, 1867, in Senate Executive Document 14, 40 Cong. 2 Sess., pp. 82–83; McCulloch to Linderman, Treasury Department, December 23, 26, 27, 1867, all in McCulloch Papers, Lilly Library of Indiana University; Sherman to McCulloch, Washington, December 23, 1867, and McCulloch to Linderman, Treasury, December 26, 1867, in NA RG 104, General Correspondence of the Mint (hereinafter cited GCM), box 113; Linderman to McCulloch, Philadelphia, January 2, 1868, NA RG 104, to Sec. Treas.

cents, from the list of American coins, limit the legal-tender power of all other silver coins to ten dollars, and make them equiponderant with the Latin Union silver coins. In short, the bill would have put the United States on the gold standard, demonetized silver as a standard, and unified American gold and silver coinage with the French.

Sherman's reasoning, as he reported it to the Senate, followed the assumptions and rhetoric of bullionist liberalism. The idea of a common monetary standard among nations, he said, had often been discussed and its usefulness conceded. But it was essential that such a standard be "fixed and invariable," "for the value of property and all internal commerce adapts itself to the intrinsic value of the gold and silver in the prescribed standard." The United States, if his bill were adopted, would share in the general benefit a unified standard would give to all civilized nations, and it would benefit specially because it was a major gold producer (he did not mention that the U. S. was becoming an even bigger silver producer); moreover, since gold was not then circulating, the timing was ideal for the shift. In a patriotic appeal, Sherman stressed that

The single standard of gold is an American idea, yielded reluctantly by France and other countries, where silver is the chief standard of value. The impossible attempt to maintain two standards of value has given rise to nearly all the debasement of coinage of the last two centuries. . . . The opportunity is now offered to the United States to secure a common international standard in the metal most valuable of all others—best adapted for coinage, mainly the product of our own country, and in conformity with a policy so constantly urged by our statesmen, and now agreed to by the oldest and wealthiest nations of the world.

What about silver?

The provisions in regard to silver coinage are urged by the Director of the Mint to secure harmony between the present market value of gold and silver; but this coinage can be regulated hereafter by the varying values of the two metals and without disturbing the sole legal standard of value [gold] for large sums.[9]

9. Senate Report 117, 40 Cong. 2 Sess., pp. 1–5.

Yet Sherman's gold standard bill did not get far. On June 9, 1868, he reported it back to the Senate, together with a minority report by Senator Edwin D. Morgan of New York. Morgan had four major objections. One, Browne's report predicted rises in gold and silver production: with bullion more abundant, and hence depreciating, public creditors were facing a loss. Before a bill was passed, more ought to be known of the effect of increased bullion production on purchasing power. Second, Sherman's bill wanted to devalue the dollar by three-and-a-half cents, and this loss to the tune of about $100 million, especially on top of depreciation through production increases, would be thoroughly unfair to creditors. Third, the bill failed to provide ways to keep silver in circulation as minor coinage and for Asian and Latin-American trade. Finally, the public had not been sufficiently heard on the whole question.[10]

Morgan's objections apparently had effect, for Sherman decided not to press for any action on S. 217. He ordered printed five thousand copies of the bill, and also the reports of Ruggles on the Paris Conference and Browne on bullion production prospects, and the bill died. Still, Sherman had learned something: the next time he or anyone presented a gold standard bill, some provision would have to be made to keep silver in circulation but get rid of it as a legal tender and standard. Any payment of debts with a devalued gold dollar was out of the question. Very perceptibly, the overriding reason for putting the United States on the gold standard shifted at this point or came out into the open: talk of the liberal and civilizing project of unifying the coinages of the leading nations lessened, while the focus was more and more on the stability of gold, its "intrinsic" value, the impracticality of bimetallism because of the fluctuations in silver, and the need to protect the public credit by effectuating the monetary stability that only gold could provide.[11]

Months elapsed before there was any further real action on a coinage bill. In the meantime, the money question became a

10. *Ibid.*, pp. 9–13.
11. *Senate Journal,* 40 Cong. 2 Sess., pp. 465–66; *Congressional Globe,* 40 Cong. 2 Sess., p. 2959; both June 9, 1868.

great issue in national politics for the first time in the presidential campaign of 1868. The national platform of the Democrats, though not Governor Horatio Seymour, their presidential candidate, offered the "Pendleton Plan" of repaying the federal debt in greenbacks, while the more discreet Republicans, satisfying themselves with an ambiguous plank promising to protect creditors and debtors alike, tried to keep the campaign focused on Reconstruction. In the lame-duck session following the election, Republicans began a more openly hard-money position than they had before, and after President Grant and the Republicans took charge of the Executive Branch and the Congress in early March, 1869, they passed the Public Credit Act declaring the bonds payable in coin unless expressly stipulated otherwise.

The Congressional session that began in the spring of 1869 also saw Senator Sherman re-introduce a gold and silver coinage bill. But Sherman did not push hard for its passage. Warned perhaps by Senator Morgan's opposition of the year before and the drift of his party toward harder money in the intervening months, Sherman seemed content simply to get the proposal into the hopper. There were, moreover, several indications in 1869 that a threat of silver pouring into the market and the Mint had slackened considerably. The head of the San Francisco Mint had reported to his superiors that silver dollars were in no demand for Oriental trade; another Treasury investigation of mining conditions in 1868 was considerably less sanguine about silver production increases than Browne had been; the Mint Director reported a definite leveling-off of silver coinage in fiscal 1869 from the increases of the previous three years.[12]

But if silver demonetization seemed a little less urgent in 1869 than it had before, it was just as desirable as ever. Mint officials and other Treasury-appointed experts, all of them utterly convinced, as one of them said, that "gold is our only standard," continued working toward a new coinage law. The

12. John Hewston, Jr., to W. E. DuBois, San Francisco, June 8, 1868, in NA RG 104, GCM box 114; House Executive Document 54, 40 Cong. 3 Sess. (report of Rossiter W. Raymond on western mining), pp. 5, 50–51; House Executive Document 2, 41 Cong. 2 Sess. (report of the Secretary of the Treasury for 1869), pp. 367–68.

primary object of such a law was to put the United States clearly on the single standard of gold. Other desirable objects, but secondary and dispensable ones, were to provide for a subsidiary coinage made from American products (silver and/or nickel), and to unify the American coinage as far as possible with European to form an international unit.[13]

None of these officials, with one outstanding exception, seemed to be acting clearly on the expectation that silver prices were threatening to drop so drastically as to drive out gold as long as the country remained on the bimetallic standard. They were convinced gold monometallists, but their desire for a new law rested more on long-held beliefs than on immediate events. The great exception was Henry Linderman, the Mint Director until April 1869 and a close adviser of Secretary of the Treasury Boutwell for the next four years.[14]

A few years after the Act of 1873 became law, Linderman published a small book about the money question, and in it he stated that the act's provisions "place the United States upon the single gold standard. The silver dollar had already become obsolete in fact; the law of 1873 merely conformed to that fact. This legislation was a continuation and consummation of that which took place in 1834 and 1853, which had for their object the use of gold as the principle [sic] money of coin payments in this country." He also had no doubt at all that if the 1873 Act had not been passed, government bonds would have depreciated very badly as silver declined, and any refunding at lower interest rates would have been impossible.[15] Was this

13. Elias Hacket Derby to McCulloch, Philadelphia Mint, February 9, 1869, NA RG 104, to Sec. Treas.; W. E. DuBois to Linderman, Philadelphia Mint, April 6, 1869, in NA RG 104, GCM box 117; DuBois article in *Bankers' Magazine* (September 1869), ("This is not a scheme for debasing the standard of value. Its only object is to restore silver upon such a basis, under legal sanctions, as will enable it to keep its subsidiary place, whether the chief currency be paper, as it is now, or gold, as we hope it soon will be."), 176; Mint Director's Report for fiscal 1869, in House Executive Document 2, 41 Cong. 2 Sess., pp. 348–50.

14. As a Democrat, Linderman lost the directorship when the Republicans took over with Grant, but neither Boutwell nor other policymakers had any desire to dispense with his services entirely.

15. Linderman, *Money and Legal Tender in the United States* (New York: G. P. Putnam's Sons, 1878), pp. 44–45.

hindsight? Or was Linderman reasoning along the same lines in 1869?

Linderman made his motives crystal-clear to no one in 1869. But he certainly was a consistent advocate of policies perfectly consonant with his later reasoning; he was expert in metallurgy, mining technology, and monetary theory; he had been keeping in close touch with British, German, and French developments regarding coinage law, mint practice, and bullion markets; he must have known that the price of silver had slithered below the French parity ratio for the last time in April, 1867; he personally investigated, at Boutwell's behest, American western mines and the branch mints in the early fall of 1869, as J. Ross Browne and others had done before him. If William Stanley Jevons had been able to predict the end of the long silver bull market in the spring of 1867, it could not have escaped Linderman two and a half years later.[16] In short, there is circumstantial evidence to support, and none to deny, the view that Linderman favored a gold standard law in 1869 *because* a decline in silver prices, and hence a severe threat to the stability of values, especially bond values, was in the offing.

By late 1869, then, every important policy-maker was looking toward the drafting and enactment of a gold standard law. Secretaries Seward and McCulloch had favored it during the Johnson administration; Senator Sherman had already brought it before Congress; Mint and Treasury officials were working assiduously to back it up with expert knowledge and detailed proposals. The next move was up to Secretary of the Treasury George S. Boutwell.

Boutwell, probably in late November, took the first step along the legislative path that led directly to the "Crime of '73." The Secretary commissioned Deputy Comptroller of the Currency John Jay Knox, with Linderman assisting, to draft a

16. B. F. Stevens to Linderman, Despatch Agency of the U. S., London, September 21, 1867, and August 11, 1868, in NA RG 104, GCM, boxes 113 and 115; Henry B. Russell, *International Monetary Conferences* (New York and London: Harper & Brothers Publishers, 1898), p. 32; Boutwell to Linderman, Treasury Department, October 27, 1869, in NA RG 104, Fair Copies of Letters from Treasury to Mint.

comprehensive coinage bill that would go to Congress at the next session. Knox and Linderman had been in frequent contact with each other over coinage matters for two years at the very least. Five years younger than Linderman, Knox had Treasury credentials nearly as good: a clerkship in the Department during the Civil War, practical banking experience, charge of the Treasury-Mint correspondence just after the War, a special investigator for McCulloch of the branch mints in 1866, and Deputy Comptroller of the Currency (supervising the national banks) since 1867.[17]

Knox went to work immediately. According to his official report, he drew up a draft bill in December 1869, sent out the draft for comment to more than a dozen present and former Mint and Treasury officials, received replies in January, February, and March, 1870, re-drafted the bill, and sent it to Boutwell, who submitted it to Congress on April 25, 1870. The first draft provided for a silver dollar of 384 grains, just twice the weight of the debased half-dollar provided for in the existing law passed in 1853, and with its legal-tender powers limited to five dollars. Linderman wrote Knox, perhaps for the record, that it would be better to discontinue the silver dollar altogether rather than to let it circulate even as a debased coin, on the grounds that "The gold dollar is really the legal unit and measure of value," and that silver did not circulate anyway since it was undervalued; the silver dollar was "of no practical use whatever." This comment was either illogical or disingenuous. But despite protests from a few of the other commentators, who wanted some kind of silver dollar (and silver five-cent and three-cent pieces, which the bill proposed also to abolish) kept on the coinage list for foreign trade and because silver was an important American product, Linderman's view prevailed.

The revised draft which Boutwell sent to Congress included no silver dollar at all. The omission cannot possibly have been casual: Knox inserted into the draft three paragraphs of com-

17. Knox-Linderman letters, 1867–68, in NA RG 104, GCM, boxes 112, 114; Knox to Mint Director James Pollock, Treasury Department, November 8, 1869, in *ibid.*, box 120; House Executive Document 4, 39 Cong. 2 Sess. (Report of the Secretary of the Treasury), pp. 29, 255–67.

ment on the history of the gold and silver dollars and on "Silver Dollar—Its Discontinuance as a Standard," glosses that he made on no other provision of the lengthy bill. The silver dollar was not only discontinued as a coin (though Knox left open the possibility of a silver dollar for Oriental trade only) but as a monetary standard and unit. "The present laws . . .," Knox explained, "authorize both a gold-dollar unit and a silver-dollar unit, differing from each other in intrinsic value. The present gold-dollar piece is made the dollar unit in the proposed bill, and the silver dollar piece is discontinued."

Some of the bill's other provisions are worth noting because either they tied it to past coinage developments or they would affect in one way or another its course through Congress. The bill proposed to discontinue silver coins of five and three cents and replace them with nickel ones. It would repeal the charge made by the Mint for coining gold, in the hope that American-produced gold bullion would stay in America rather than "flying," as Knox put it, to the British Mint, which had no coinage charge, or the French Mint, where the charge was lower than the prevailing American one. Rather than having to accept and coin all silver presented to the U. S. Mint, which had been the practice, the amount to be coined would be at the discretion of Mint officials and only in exchange for gold at the par value. All of the Mint branches, including Philadelphia, would be centralized under a Director officed at the Treasury Department in Washington. As for metric weights, the bill recommended (but did not require) them, and Boutwell's covering letter pointed out that the existing dime needed only a slight reduction to equal one-tenth of the French silver five-franc piece; as for international coinage unification, "The United States would undoubtedly agree to any system of international coinage . . . first agreed upon by England and France," among which the metric system was the most advantageous.

But these were perfunctory nods indeed to the activities of the past several years in behalf of international unification of coinage, weights, and measures. This was a gold standard bill, one even more geared to American interests than Sherman's bill of 1868. It dropped the silver dollar, reduced the legal-tender powers of the remaining silver coins to one dollar, gave the Mint Director full power to limit silver purchases as he saw fit, and valued any such silver purchases in gold. This was getting rid of the silver standard with a vengeance—a singular degree of attention to a problem that ostensibly was of no practical concern.[18]

The Knox-Linderman report pointed out that the silver dollar, even at one to fifteen and a half, stood to gold at a premium of more than a dollar and three cents (at one to sixteen it would have been higher). They made no reference to the possibility of a fall in silver values. The direct evidence, then, is that they wanted the silver dollar dropped as a full tender and a unit of account (and possibly retained solely as a "commercial dollar" circulating abroad) for the purpose of the stabilization of values—resting them on the "intrinsic value" of gold. If this is what Knox and Linderman were aiming for, they were ignorant and obtuse with regard to possible shifts in the supply and hence in the market values of bullion.

But it was generally known to experts everywhere that silver stocks were increasing and silver values were declining. There is every probability that both Knox and Linderman understood this. Such knowledge does not mean they were not interested in stabilization via gold monometallism—in fact it reinforces it—but it does mean they were something less than frank in their adducing of reasons for it.

Even before Boutwell submitted the revised draft of the coinage bill to the House and Senate, there were indications that these bodies had ideas of their own and were not willing to adopt the Treasury draft either quickly or in its pristine state. Congressman William D. Kelley, the Philadelphia Republican and disciple of Henry C. Carey, who incidentally had long been acquainted with Linderman, introduced a bill on February 7, 1870, to establish an international metric coinage, as he had

18. The revised draft of the bill, together with covering letters from Knox and Boutwell and correspondence early in 1870 that Knox solicited from experts, is in Senate Executive Document 132 and House Executive Document 307, both 41 Cong. 2 Sess., dated April 25, 1870. The draft of the bill as it went to Boutwell, with Knox's explanatory letter, is in NA RG 104, Fair Copies of Letters from Treasury to Mint.

done in 1869. Congressman Samuel Hooper of Massachusetts introduced a coinage bill of his own on March 16 embodying the unification plan of Samuel Bulkley Ruggles and the Paris Conference of 1867. Kelley and Hooper threw expert witnesses, including Ruggles, at each other in hearings of the House Committee on Coinage, Weights, and Measures from February through April. Sherman, meanwhile, was in contact with the British Chancellor of the Exchequer, Robert Lowe, with regard to unifying British and American coinage, while at the same time Sherman's Senate Finance Committee received a private petition calling elaborately for French-oriented international coinage based on the metric system. On top of all this, Boutwell and Knox solicited further expert opinion on the coinage bill, apparently at the behest of House members, even though the "finished" draft had been submitted.[19]

By the middle of 1870, Congressional thrust toward a new coinage bill was therefore fragmented among Congressman Hooper, who leaned toward a more British version; Congressman Kelley, who favored a more metric and Gallic version; and Senator Sherman, who was probably sympathetic to any bill generally along the lines of the Treasury draft and which would pass. Throughout the spring of 1870 and into July, however, the main job of Congressional financial leaders was to pass legislation refunding the Civil War debt and stabilizing the national bank note and greenback currency. This was ultimately done, and a Currency Act and a Funding Act did pass during the second week of July. But the battle was so exhausting that the differences over the coinage bill could not possibly have

19. Minute Book and Docket Book, House Committee on Coinage, Weights, and Measures, 1870, in NA, Legislative Branch; Kelley to Linderman, Philadelphia, May 30?, 1868, in NA RG 104, GCM, box 114; McCulloch to E. B. Elliott, Treasury Department, January 2, 1869, in NA, Record Group 56 (Secretary of the Treasury records), Letters from Secretary XXII: 497; Kelley to McCulloch, Washington, February 14, 1869, NA RG 56, to Secretary from Congress, box 60; Hooper to Mint Director, Washington, March 17, 1870, in NA RG 104, GCM, box 121; Benjamin Moran to Sherman, London, January 8 and May 26, 1870, in Sherman Papers, Library of Congress; petition from Universal Decimal Weight and Measure and Coinage Association, in Senate Finance Committee papers, May 16, 1870, in NA, Legislative Branch (41A-H7.1); House Executive Document 307, 41 Cong. 2 Sess., "B".

been resolved. Sherman did not even report the bill until Congress reconvened the following December. In all probability Sherman and Boutwell saw the coinage bill as a necessary adjunct to the Funding and Currency Acts, since only the coinage bill would assure that the "coin" into which paper currency would be convertible when specie payments were resumed, and with which the refunded bonds would be paid, would be gold coin, not gold and silver. But the coinage bill had to wait. Sherman, Boutwell, and other orthodox-thinking men could nevertheless console themselves that of all the versions and proposals for revising the coinage laws of the United States, not one called for the retention of the silver standard. The overwhelming body of policy-making opinion in the United States supported the single standard of gold.

Over four years had gone by since Sherman, Kasson, Ruggles, and McCulloch started the process, in the context of international coinage unification, by which the United States would join the gold standard countries. Two and a half more years would pass until the Coinage Act finally became law in February, 1873. But those years were marked chiefly by a struggle within Congress over the kind of act that would be passed, and by steadily increasing visibility of a silver production surplus that threatened to shake fundamentally the money and credit structure of the country, if the country remained officially bimetallic.

Silver abundance, which had slacked off in 1869, was more evident than ever in 1870. Even as Knox and Linderman were putting the finishing touches on their revised draft of the coinage bill in March of 1870, Mint Director Pollock was writing Boutwell and Knox that "The deposits of silver bullion are increasing, as also the demand for silver coinage," and he sought authority to raise the Mint's fund for buying silver. Just after the bill went to Congress, Linderman set off for London to inspect minting, bullion, and refining conditions, as he had done in the American West the preceding fall, and promised to keep Boutwell informed; Linderman already knew of one refinery that was "overcrowded with silver ores." The London *Economist* reported later in 1870 that the Royal Mint had become overstocked with silver during the year, and Rossiter Raymond, the U. S. Treasury's new mining commissioner, described at length the discovery of new silver ores at the Comstock, which developed into one of the area's greatest strikes.[20]

When Sherman presented the coinage bill to the Senate on January 9, 1871, he did so in a complicated context. Silver production was increasing, and the German and other Central European demonetizations of silver were in the offing. The business cycle was rising, and American government bonds authorized by the Funding Act of July 14, 1870, were about to be floated on an investment market apparently intrigued more with railroad securities and the bonds of other countries. If the whole refunding and currency-stabilization scheme that Sherman and the Treasury had inched through a discordant Congress in the 1870 session were not to collapse, the public credit would have to be shored up in every possible way. The coinage bill was gaining urgency.

The Senate dealt with it quickly and somewhat cavalierly. Sherman offered it with the assurance that "it does not adopt any new principles," pointing out that it did not provide for international coinage unification "because that is not a codification of the existing law, but a great and important and radical change of the law." Unification would have been much less "great and important and radical" than the silver demonetization it actually contained, but Sherman chose not to discuss the silver provisions. The only significant debate was over the charge to be made by the Mint for coining gold. The Senators from gold-producing California were able to have the coinage charge stricken out, over Sherman's strenuous objections. On January 10, 1871, the Senate passed the bill as amended, 36 for and 14 against, with Sherman in the minority.

"Pig-Iron" Kelley entered the bill in the House of Representatives the next day, had it sent to his Coinage, Weights, and Measures Committee, and on February 25 reported it and

20. Pollock to Boutwell, Mint, March 7, 1870, and Pollock to Knox, Mint, March 10, 1870, in NA RG 104, to Sec. Treas. box 6; Linderman to Boutwell, New York, April 26, 1870, in *ibid.; Economist,* December 3, 1870, 1456; House Executive Document 10, 42 Cong. 1 Sess., p. 93.

had it recommitted. It never re-emerged during the Forty-first Congress. Kelley finally brought it to the floor in the second session of the Forty-second Congress eleven months later, on January 9, 1872. The House debated it that day and the next, and Kelley's floor management was so inept that he almost managed to get the bill killed entirely. The debate over the section providing for a new Mint Director, and what his salary would cost, dragged on so long that one exasperated member moved to strike the bill's enacting clause; this motion actually passed twice until a roll call defeated it and kept the bill alive.

The rest of the discussion was even more bizarre. Kelley assured his colleagues, as Sherman had done the year before in the Senate, that international coinage unification (which he had once supported vociferously) did not appear in the bill because "I was charged with a bill that looked only to the codification of the mint laws, or mainly that, [and] I did not feel it well to interject into that bill any of my own peculiar views." The silver and gold coins were just the same as before, claimed Kelley, and so were the minor coins except that more of them were to be of nickel.

The word "nickel" touched off a very short fuse. Several Congressmen were convinced that Kelley was simply trying to protect the interests of a fellow Philadelphian, Joseph Wharton, whose business interests included a nickel refinery in Camden, New Jersey, which had been supplying nickel to the Mint for years at a price above the open market and in large quantities (so great that the Chief Coiner wrote the Mint Director in late 1870 that "We have so many years stock of nickel on hand, that I would regard [it] as the extreme of mercantile folly for us to purchase a single pound more"). Congressman James R. Mc-Cormick of Missouri, a Democrat, told the House that "My impression is that the primary object of this bill is to affect the manner in which nickel shall be purchased. . . . There are in the United States more places producing nickel than the State of Pennsylvania." Missouri was one of them, and McCormick moved that the bill be recommitted with instructions to report it only when it provided for competitive bidding on any nickel bought by the Mint. The bill went back to committee.[21]

By the time it was debated again on the floor of the House, on April 9, 1872, Kelley had bowed out as floor leader. Samuel Hooper, probably the most astute and most experienced of House Republican financial solons, brought out a bill changed in several important respects. Since Kelley's botch in January, Hooper had not only kept his signals straight with Boutwell, listened one more time to Samuel B. Ruggles plead for international coinage unification on the gold standard, but also solicited outside opinion.

Here was born the curious twist of the agrarian legend of the "Crime of '73" that Ernest Seyd, acting as agent for London and continental bankers (especially the Rothschilds) and armed with £100,000, bribed the Congress into demonetizing silver. What happened was that Hooper sent a copy of the bill to Alfred Latham, a Director of the Bank of England, for comment. Latham forwarded it to Ernest Seyd, by then a leading bullion merchant and writer on money. Seyd replied directly to Hooper from his offices in Princes Street in the City of London —there is no evidence that he was within three thousand miles of Washington in 1872—in a long letter. Seyd recognized that the most important section of the bill was the one dropping the silver dollar and hence the silver standard. Referring Hooper to an enclosed copy of a book he had written in 1871 on American coinage, Seyd repeated his long-held and very strenuous *objection* to the demonetization of silver: demonetization would lead only to "idleness, poverty, demoralization, and crime." The United States should resume the free coinage of silver, he appealed to Hooper, and continue to seek international agreement on a universal silver unit to circulate concurrently with gold. Seyd, in short, was a thoroughgoing international bimetal-

21. *Congressional Globe,* 42 Cong. 2 Sess., pp. 322–28, 336–40 (January 9, 10, 1872); *House Journal,* 42 Cong. 2 Sess., pp. 127–35 (same dates); Minute Book of Coinage Weights and Measures Committee, 1871, in NA, Legislative Branch; James C. Booth to Pollock, Mint, October 30, 1870, in NA RG 104, GCM box 121 (on Wharton's nickel and the Mint see also Pollock to Boutwell, Mint, October 15, 1869; Boutwell to Linderman, Treasury, April 5, 1869; Knox to Linderman, July 12, 1867; McCulloch to Linderman, May 2, 1867; Wharton-Mint draft agreement, January 8, 1867, all in NA RG 104, GCM boxes 111–120.

list and always had been.

Of course silver demonetization had completely won the day long before Seyd ever wrote to Hooper. If there was some well-bankrolled plot by European financiers, the bagman could much more easily have been Linderman, who visited Germany and England in late 1871. But there is no evidence for this and no need for it to have happened in order for silver demonetization to have taken place. If Seyd's advice did anything, it brought silver *back* into the bill to a place it had not had since Knox's original draft of late 1869: when Hooper reported it back to the House on April 9, 1872, it contained a silver dollar of 384 grains, less than the old standard but very close to the five-franc piece and just twice the existing U. S. silver fifty-cent piece. Its tender powers were limited to five dollars, so that it was no longer a standard; but it was at least available for trade purposes, as a way of consuming domestically-produced silver, and (probably most importantly) served as a small step toward universal coinage.[22]

Hooper, commenting on the bill section by section before the House, stated bluntly that the bill made the gold dollar the "unit of value" and took that property away from the silver dollar, "which by law is now the legally declared unit of value," because silver was worth about $1.03 in gold and tended to fluctuate. Congressman William L. Stoughton of Michigan seconded this: "The value of silver depends, in a great measure, upon the fluctuations of the market, and the supply and demand. Gold is practically the standard of value among all civilized nations, and the time has come in this country when the gold dollar should be distinctly declared to be the coin representative of the money unit." Clarkson Potter of New York agreed, as did others. Apparently it crossed none of their minds that under a true bimetallic standard, each metal was measurable in terms of the other, and not just silver in terms of

22. Boutwell to Hooper, Treasury Department, February 3, 1872, in NA RG 104, Fair copies of letters to Mint; Senate Miscellaneous Document 29, 53 Cong. 1 Sess.; Ernest Seyd, *Suggestions in Reference to the Metallic Currency of the United States of America* (London: Trübner & Co., 1871), pp. 55–58, 207; Boutwell to Linderman, Treasury Department, October 17, 1871, in NA RG 104, Fair copies of letters to Mint.

gold; if silver fluctuated in terms of gold, it was just as accurate to say that gold fluctuated in terms of silver. But all of them were so closely tied to contemporary commercial practice, in which gold was indeed the standard for large transactions and the sole standard of the two greatest European trading nations of the day, Britain and Germany, that gold was to them the one true standard and silver could never be anything more than a satellite of it. The merchant prince Hooper had actually confessed to Alfred Latham that he simply did not understand the "double valuation."

One thing puzzled Potter: since America was using neither silver nor gold, and specie resumption was some time away, why change the silver dollar just then? A pointed question. Not one participant in the debate so much as implied that silver prices were dropping and could well drop further. The only answer was that the debasement of the silver dollar, and other features of the bill, would help to prevent the exportation of the increasing domestic silver product, a patriotic motive that had been suggested in earlier debates.

Partly because Kelley managed to get into a fracas with a New York Congressman over the bill's substitution of nickel for silver in the five-cent piece, it was recommitted once more. But Hooper brought it back on May 27, 1872, promised that nickel purchases would be competitive and no new small coins would be made, succeeded in cutting off further debate, and the bill passed comfortably, without a roll call, 110-13.[23]

The patching up of differences and passing of the bill in the House came none too soon. By the time Sherman was able to bring it before the Senate the following January (1873), silver was finally and clearly plunging downward, and the pressure to demonetize was great. Norway had begun selling silver as far back as 1869, Sweden and the Netherlands were switching from silver to gold monometallism in 1872, and the Imperial German gold coinage, to replace the silver of the *Länder,* was legal reality. The *Economist* reported in November, 1872, that silver was at its lowest price in twenty years, and blamed the German monetary changes. German thalers and Mexican dol-

23. *Congressional Globe,* 42 Cong. 2 Sess., pp. 2304–43, 3882–83.

lars were rolling into the New York Assay Office of the Mint for recoinage, and the demand for newly minted silver dollars kept increasing. Pollock had told Boutwell the previous February of the "surprising production of silver" and great amounts of it coming into the Mint for coinage, and indeed the curves of silver production and dollar coinage were careening upwards.[24]

Not only was this happening, but Boutwell and Linderman knew it was happening and understood the consequences. Their response was to continue to urge passage of the gold monometallist coinage bill, and to have included in it a heavy, 420-grain silver dollar, which was to circulate in Oriental trade but not domestically as a standard and unit, thereby preserving the gold standard while making use of American-produced silver bullion. The authorship of this non-standard "trade dollar" was claimed variously by Boutwell, Linderman, certain private citizens in California, and had in fact been suggested by Senator Morgan of New York in his minority report on Sherman's gold standard bill of 1868.

Whatever its ultimate source, it was part of the bill as Sherman reported it to the Senate in January, 1873. By that time, Linderman had made another survey of the branch Mints in the West and reported to Boutwell that not only increased American production, but demonetization in Germany and other countries, inevitably presaged a "serious decline and further apparent depreciation in the value of silver." Boutwell,

24. *Economist,* November 9, 1872, 1365; Thomas C. Acton to Pollock, New York Assay Office, September 11, 1872, in NA RG 104, GCM box 126; Pollock to Boutwell, Mint, February 6, 1872, in NA RG 104, to Sec. Treas.

The following figures are for fiscal years, from Mint Director's Report, 1872, Appendix D, and Secretary of the Treasury Report, 1872, p. 442:

YEAR	DOLLAR VALUE OF SILVER PRODUCED	SILVER DOLLARS COINED (PHILA.)
(1858–67 annual average)	——	75,900
1868	986,000	55,000
1869	902,000	331,000
1870	1,327,000	576,000
1871	3,652,000	658,000
1872	7,055,000	1,109,000

in his publicly available annual report to Congress of November, 1872, agreed. He warned that "As the depreciation of silver is likely to continue it is impossible to issue coin redeemable in gold without ultimate loss to the government; for when the difference becomes considerable owners will present the silver for redemption, and leave it in the hands of the government to be disposed of subsequently at a loss." Boutwell was perfectly right. Add together declining silver values, a bimetallic standard, and Gresham's Law, and the sum was a run on the Treasury's gold and ruination of the public credit. The remedy was equally clear: demonetize silver as a standard while coining it for trade with countries who sought it, such as China.[25]

Sherman moved the bill through the Senate expertly. With regard to silver, he pointed out only that the minor silver coins were changed slightly to be equiponderant with the Latin Union five-franc silver piece. The only serious argument came from Senator Casserly of California, who wanted the coinage charge on gold removed to encourage gold imports and encourage the export of "this silver which we do not want and which before a great while may be at an absolute discount on our hands." Nevada's Senator Stewart, who in later years claimed he and the silver interests of his state had been duped, was present and awake but made no effort to defend silver. The bill passed without a division. After a House-Senate conference, in which Hooper and his colleagues agreed to the trade dollar passed by the Senate, the bill was finally approved and was signed by President Grant on February 12, 1873.[26]

Thus the "Crime of '73." Twenty years later Boutwell stated in an article in the Boston *Herald,* quoted in the Senate by Senator Dolph of Oregon, that after 1860 "The difference in favor of silver [over gold in the dollar] diminished gradually, and in 1872 the difference had disappeared. At that time the power drill had been invented and its value established. The

25. Report of the Secretary of the Treasury for 1872, House Executive Document 2, 42 Cong. 3 Sess., pp. xi–xii; "The Production of Gold and Silver", Linderman-Torrey report, November 1872, *Bankers' Magazine* (March 1873), pp. 710–12.
26. *Congressional Globe,* 42 Cong. 3 Sess., pp. 661–74, 721, 742, 815, 860, 871, 1150, 1214, 1282, 1364.

use of dynamite was well understood, and the number and richness of the silver mines in the Rocky Mountains justified the conclusion [which Sherman, Linderman and others would also have rested on European events] that silver would deteriorate in value with each succeeding year. On this theory of the then future my policy was based. We were then on a gold basis as far as the use of the metals had a part in our financial affairs; we were a principal producer of gold, and the most important steps had been taken in the work of bringing the Treasury note to the standard of gold coin." [27]

Did Sherman and the others understand what they were doing when they demonetized silver as a standard? Did they understand that silver was declining and what the consequences of that decline were? They did, and apparently had since 1866 or 1867. The decline of silver, which was foreseen, threatened specie resumption and it threatened public and private contracts in the United States, especially the sale and payment of principal and interest on the public bonds. The demonetization was not undertaken to protect creditors or to give them something for nothing, but to protect instead the public credit. To a relatively minor degree, it was undertaken also to start the United States on the road to international coinage unification; to protect, in one way or another, American producers of gold, nickel, *and* (by the trade dollar) silver; to provide Linderman with a job (he became Mint director in Washington, over Pollock, under the new Act); to place the American currency system in conformity with natural laws, supply and demand, the currency of civilized and progressive nations.

Its motivation was very complex. But a plot to defraud debtors was no more among the motivating factors than was the protection and encouragement of farmers and laborers through a policy of abundant money. The act was one more step in the Sherman-Republican policy of monetary stabilization and specie resumption. As such it was deflationary, but not, in its main thrust, malfeasant.

27. *Congressional Record*, XXV (August 8, 1893), p. 222.

6

Remonetization
and Rhetoric

~~~~~~

THE COINAGE ACT of 1873 attracted little attention around the country at the time it was passed; extraordinarily little, compared to the twenty-year clamor over its effects. The chief reason for this was not conspiratorial surreptitiousness during the process of its passage, because anyone could have followed the *Congressional Globe* or read the public documents, but rather the failure of nearly everyone except Treasury and Congressional policy-makers to anticipate silver's decline, together with the nearly total agreement of these policy-makers, whatever their other differences, on the need to put the United States on the gold standard.

By 1876 these two conditions had disappeared. Silver prices had dropped sharply and obviously, and for the first time, but not the last, policy-makers were splitting on the question of the appropriate monetary standard. Not only was gold monometallism forced on the defensive, but its underpinnings in utilitarian liberalism came under sharp attack from a revitalized and increasingly aggressive philosophy of producerism. The upshot was the partial remonetization of silver by Congress, and the forging of two tough, brittle rhetorics—of hard money and soft—in the political society at large. These developments took place between early 1876 and early 1878.

Changes in context since mid-1873 were critically important in bringing these developments about. There was, of course, the world-wide depression; it brought not only tight money but provoked certain previously benign groups (especially agrarians) into cries for relief, especially through more abundant currency. Silver, cheapened progressively by the Latin Union's suspension of silver coinage, India's drop in demand, and increased production, was an obvious and available remedy, if only the law of 1873 could be changed.

Politics also played a part. After a disastrous debate on national bank note and greenback expansion in the spring of 1874, President Grant sided with hard-money extremists in the Republican party and vetoed a very mildly inflationary bill which embodied the minimum demands of large segments, particularly Midwesterners, of the party. The Republicans went into the congressional campaign of 1874 not only facing voter ire over the depression, but rent asunder over currency policy. The Democrats—to many Republicans the party of Andrew Johnson, secession, copperheadism, and Southern recalcitrance —not only won control of the House of Representatives for the first time since pre-war days, but threatened to win the presidency in 1876. The Democrats had divisions of their own between hard- and soft-money wings, but for various reasons they were much more likely to entertain "heretical notions on money" than the Republicans. In what was a crucial episode in late nineteenth-century party politics, Sherman responded to this threat during the last Republican-controlled session of Congress before the Democratic deluge by hammering out a currency bill which succeeded in uniting virtually every Senate Republican and most of those in the House. This bill, which became the Specie Resumption Act of 1875, gave an increase in national bank notes to the softer-money wing, more subsidiary silver coinage to representatives of silver-producing states, and the promise of specie resumption in four years to the primarily Northeastern hard-money extremists. Even this successful appeal by Sherman for Republicans to mute monetary differences in favor of party unity, and which allowed them at least to avoid going into the next presidential election at each others' throats, did not completely prevent the Republican monetary coalition from becoming partly unstuck during the next three eventful years.

With Democrats controlling the House, without a threat of

cloture hanging over the expression of unorthodox opinions, the Forty-fourth Congress quickly became the scene of a debate on monetary policy perhaps wider-ranging than any since Jackson's day. By July and August, 1876, with the presidential election only weeks away and very much in the legislators' minds, two bills reached the floor: one to repeal the pledge in the Specie Resumption Act of 1875 to resume payments on January 1, 1879, and the other to restore the unlimited coinage of the 412½-grain silver dollar and thus make the United States bimetallic again. Argument over these two issues—resumption repeal and free silver—was to go on for more than two years. Often the same Congressmen supported both measures, but free silver had an advantage over the more greenbackish resumption repeal in that it was not only inflationary and satisfactory to producerites but could appeal also to Congressmen whose fundamental bullionism still nagged them. The response of the gold-monometallist leadership, which had never opposed silver as a non-standard coinage metal, was simple: remonetization within strict limits and, if possible, an international agreement on a ratio at which silver would be supported.

Senator Sherman, in advance of the pack as usual, was already working along these lines. He supported legislation passed on April 17 and July 22, 1876, authorizing and requiring the Treasury to buy silver, issue it as subsidiary coin, replace fractional paper and some greenbacks with it, and thus put the country eventually on a specie-silver basis for minor coins. At one point he called this process "the first and most difficult step" toward specie resumption. At the same time he was very careful not to give silver any status whatever as a standard, and the law of July 22 removed the domestic legal-tender powers of the silver trade dollar entirely. During those same months he corresponded with the Treasury and saw through Congress a concurrent resolution to bring about unification of British and American gold coinage and to set up an international monetary conference to devise a world-wide gold-silver ratio (which would have amounted to an international support level).

As he wrote later in the year to Hugh McCulloch, Sherman abhorred free silver, which would "not only impair the public credit but would lead to great derangement of business and practically establish the single standard of silver." But he had nothing against the silver dollar if it was carefully controlled; "I am in favor of issuing it and a very large sum of subsidiary coins and with them reducing the greenback circulation, making the silver dollar a legal tender to the same extent that U. S. notes are now a legal tender, but excepting expressly customs duties and the public debts." Thus, "it will like silver change in England be kept at the standard of gold when we come to specie payments." Linderman's views were much the same; it was beginning to dawn on him, as on others, that perhaps gold was appreciating, that silver depreciation was not the whole of the problem; silver ought to be used under conditions that in no way threatened the gold standard. Gold was civilized, European, practical; silver was barbaric, Asian, cumbersome—hence gold monometallism was inviolable; but silver had its uses (and was certainly creating its pressures).[1]

These views ultimately and largely prevailed. But they represented simply the old orthodoxies under pressure. In the Congress, particularly in the House, views diverged. Free silver, sponsored by William D. Kelley, Republican, and Richard P. Bland of Missouri, Democrat, passed the House late in July, 1876, and repeal of the resumption-day clause in the Act of 1875 passed on August 5. On the latter day Bland and Congressman Abram Hewitt of New York, the National Chairman of Bland's own party, clashed bitterly. The rhetoric they used was to become the rhetoric of the opposing sides of the money question for twenty years.

"Silver Dick" Bland did not mince words. The Public Credit Act of 1869 and the Coinage Act of 1873, promising repayment of the government bonds in coin rather than the paper they were bought with, and then changing "coin" to gold alone,

1. *Senate Journal,* 44 Cong. 1 Sess., pp. 566, 606; Sherman to Secretary of the Treasury B. H. Bristow, Washington, February 23, 1876, in NA RG 56, Letters of Secretary of the Treasury, box 82; Senate Miscellaneous Document 35, 44 Cong. 1 Sess.; *Congressional Record,* 44 Cong. 1 Sess., p. 3684; Sherman to McCulloch, Washington, December 21, 1876, in McCulloch Papers, Library of Congress; Mint Director's Report, in House Executive Document 2, 44 Cong. 2 Sess., pp. 296, 307, 311.

"were in the interest of stock-jobbers and speculators in Government bonds." He upheld the public credit; he accepted specie resumption. But to say that "the tax-payer must pay in gold alone would be robbery, nothing more, nothing less"; it would be changing the contract to give an enormous windfall to creditors. His bill to remonetize silver, Bland exclaimed, "is a measure in the interest of the honest yeomanry of this country."

Because a measure is for once reported to this Congress that has within it a provision for the welfare of the people of the country against the corrupt legislation that has gone on here for the last sixteen years in the interest of the moneyed lords it is here denounced as full of rascalities, and all this by the party that had perpetrated these injustices and brought corruption, fraud, infamy, and dishonor upon the country. . . . Mr. Speaker, the common people of the country cannot come to this Capitol. They are not here in your lobby. They are at home following the plow, cultivating the soil, or working in their workshops. It is the silvern [*sic*] and golden slippers of the money kings, the bankers and financiers, whose step is heard in these lobbies and who rule the finances of the country.

For the Scrooges of Wall Street, Bland's voice was that of the Ghost of Christmas-yet-to-come. His producerism was a carry-over from greenback theory, but the remedy of free silver and the rhetoric of corruption and class insolence was that of the Populism of fifteen years later. Bland was a prominent member of a new breed of monetary politicians who believed in the producer philosophy just as much as the laborite and manufacturing greenbackers of a few years before, but who could rightly claim to be just as bullionist as anyone because silver was their currency. He and other sons of the Middle Border represented constituents who were happiest with hard money, so long as it was reasonably abundant; silver appealed to them as greenbacks never could. William D. Kelley, who continued to support or sponsor free-silver bills, was even more clearly than Bland a bridge between Careyite greenbackism and free silver: in the late seventies he advocated both, and his free-silver bills appealed to soft-money House Republicans as Bland's did to Democrats.

Abram Hewitt's remonstrance against the Bland bill on August 5, 1876, must have read like a confession to Bland.

"Against this bill I am charged by the Chamber of Commerce of the City of New York to speak," declared Hewitt. The Chamber was made up as always of "the leading merchants, bankers, and manufacturers of the city of New York," who were "the jealous guardians of commercial honor." But not only these men—"money sharks" to Bland—but many others should stand fast against free silver. If silver were remonetized, mortgage-holders, "many of them ill able to bear the loss," would lose 18 percent; with public bonds payable in silver there would be a transfer "from the creditor to the debtor class of a sum greater than the entire debt of the United States." Quoting John Stuart Mill in support of gold as the only civilized standard, Hewitt was horrified at the prospect of widows and orphans losing their small competencies, laborers defrauded of wages, creditors and property-owners of all kinds bilked of their wealth, all because of the government's spineless acceptance of a depreciated dollar.[2]

Both Bland and Hewitt maintained the inviolability of the public credit, the sanctity of contracts, the ideal of "honest money." But to Hewitt the silver dollar would derange existing contracts; to Bland they had already been deranged by the Public Credit Act and the 1873 Coinage Act and remonetization would only restore the original contract. The rhetorics were practically irreconcilable, and they were hardening. What about reality? There, too, a mounting impasse. The silverites claimed accurately that tight money and long-term deflation was needlessly harsh for the many and suspiciously beneficial for a few. On the other hand, as Congressman Townsend of Pennsylvania pointed out, if Congress passed the Bland bill, "we will never to able to induce a bondholder to change another bond from a 6 percent to a 5 percent loan." To a developing country for which inflows of investment capital were essential, this consideration was impossible to avoid. As early as the summer of 1876, the battle was joined between two armies each convinced that the right was on their side, each viewing with profound alarm a future in which their enemies might prevail,

2. *Congressional Record,* 44 Cong. 1 Sess., pp. 5235–36 and appendix pp. 283–86.

and each rapidly developing a rhetoric designed not to reason with the enemy but to convince the uncommitted.

Though in 1876 the House actually passed the free-silver coinage bill and repealed the resumption-day clause, Sherman's Senate Finance Committee smothered them. Aside from legislating in April and July, 1876, to provide for more subsidiary silver coinage, the Forty-fourth Congress could agree on the money question solely to the extent of setting up a bipartisan commission to hear witnesses, study the question, and recommend legislation. The resulting United States Monetary Commission did just that for well over a year. It was the first and the last significant official occasion in the nineteenth century when the two opposing sides had the opportunity to confront and cross-examine each other. Afterwards communication never really took place. The Commission's Report went to a Congress that had already made up its mind.

Shortly after the Forty-fifth Congress convened in the fall of 1877, Bland introduced a brief, blunt bill to authorize unlimited coinage of the old standard silver dollar with full legal-tender powers. It passed the House on the same day it was introduced, November 5, by a vote of one hundred sixty-three to thirty-four. Before it appeared in the Senate, the silver forces won what appeared to be a major victory with regard to the perennial concomitant of the currency question, the method of repaying the government debt. Senator Stanley Matthews, ironically the man who took John Sherman's seat when Sherman became President Hayes' Secretary of the Treasury earlier that year, submitted a concurrent resolution declaring that since silver, as well as gold, was a monetary standard at the time of the Public Credit Act of 1869 and the Funding Act of 1870, the payment of the bonds in silver was "not in violation of the public faith, nor in derogation of the rights of the public creditor."[3] The Matthews Resolution therefore undid at one stroke the 1873 demonetization of silver with respect to the public credit. The Senate passed it, 43-22, on January 25, 1878, after short, sharp discussion; the House passed it three days later, 189-79. All that was needed were the silver dollars themselves.

3. *Congressional Record*, VII (December 6, 1877), p. 47.

At this critical juncture the Senate Finance Committee put its finger into the dike and reduced the imminent silver flood to a trickle. Senator William B. Allison, Republican of Iowa, reported Bland's free-silver bill to the Senate with two amendments: one, the crucial one, limiting the amount of silver purchasable by the Treasury to between two and four million dollars' worth monthly; the other authorizing the government to take part in an international conference to set up a world-wide gold-silver ratio. Instead of free silver, there would be limited, international bimetallism; instead of a return to the double monetary standard, gold would remain the real standard and silver would be its satellite.

Gold-monometallist diehards and free-silverites attacked Allison's version of the Bland bill from right and left, but every significant attempt to amend it failed. The Senate passed it, and the House, not without anguish, concurred in the Senate amendments. President Hayes vetoed it, never apparently having understood either the monetary technicalities or the political necessity involved, but House and Senate over-rode the veto and the Bland-Allison Act became law early in March, 1878.

A bill to repeal much of the Specie Resumption Act had passed the House in the preceding November and was still before the Senate in May. By then, however, with the Bland-Allison Act on the statute books, resumption repeal was no longer necessary as a means of stopping free silver. The repeal bill was reduced in the Senate to a provision that greenbacks would be receivable after October 1 of that year for customs duties and payment of certain government bonds; in this the House would not concur, and resumption repeal died. In the meantime, Secretary Sherman continued to accumulate a gold reserve, the premium on gold over greenbacks slid ever downward, and the resumption of specie payments took place as promised, on January 2, 1879.

With the resumption of specie payments the Reconstruction Era in American public finance ended. The Civil War debt had been refunded and reduced. The national banks and their notes had become permanent. Greenbacks still circulated, but they had become convertible into specie; despite the existence and measurable success for a few years of a national Greenback political party, the scheme of keeping the greenbacks as a permanent inconvertible paper currency had been defeated.

But the silver question, that peculiar and at first unnoticed offspring of the Reconstruction money question, would not die. Demonetized in 1873, remonetized within strict limits in 1878, the silver dollar had assumed an unshakeable position at the crux of the money question, symbolizing dishonor to its enemies, salvation to its friends.

7

Some Ramifications

TO SUMMARIZE the foregoing in the briefest of terms, the Reconstruction money question involved the gradual and successful labor of Treasury and Congressional policy-makers to refund the Civil War debt, stabilize the bank note and greenback paper currency, and provide for the resumption of specie payments on the gold standard, which necessitated the demonetization of silver.

This program was embodied in legislation by early 1875 and progressed without serious opposition until late 1875 or early 1876. Then began a powerful drive to remonetize silver. That drive achieved a very limited success in the Bland-Allison Act of early 1878, after which specie resumption took place on the gold standard. The context of these developments included, as regards other countries, a trend toward the gold standard, freer trade, and international coinage unification until the early or mid-seventies, when the fiscal policies of the major nations shifted in a nationalistic direction; in regard to the business cycle, generally prosperous times into 1873 were followed by panic and depression until the closing months of the decade; in regard to world bullion stocks, there was a subtle but discernible decline in silver prices until about 1873 and a severe and obvious drop thereafter; in regard to the ideological attitudes of policy-makers, a gold-monometallist bullionism, rooted in utilitarian liberalism, was threatened in the United States rather ineffectually before 1876 by producerite greenbackism and after 1876 rather vigorously by producerite and bullionist freesilverism.

The money question, including the silver aspect of it, developed amid these world-economic, national-economic, diplomatic, and ideological contexts. Its visible and decisive episodes were affairs of public law and administrative policy, and therefore the people most directly involved were Treasury and Congressional leaders. But these men, even when some of them were demonetizing silver, did not operate in a vacuum or on behalf of their own or a few others' private economic ends. Behind the legislative-administrative history of the money question there was a vast and intricate pattern of shifting interest-group positions and coalitions.[1]

Some of these groups were economic; certainly banking, commercial, manufacturing, laborite, and (after 1873) agricultural groups played roles, perhaps as indirect as a Congressman's fears of voter resentment, perhaps as direct as William D. Kelley's connection with Pennsylvania manufacturers or Abram Hewitt's and Samuel B. Ruggles' representation of the New York Chamber of Commerce. But among the effective groups were others not economic, or significantly so, at all: the interests of section, of party, and above all of ideology, pressed on policy-makers at every point.

It is often said of late nineteenth-century American politics that protest movements abounded because government was not responsive to many of the deepest-felt needs of the people. The outstanding example was the agrarian and silverite pressure that underlay the People's Party and took over the Democratic Party in 1896. But the notion oversimplifies and obscures the structure of American political society at that time. The term "people" is the culprit. Government and policy-makers were actually very responsive indeed to certain people, certain groups, and certain ideologies. Policy-makers shared values with some groups; were often leading spokesmen for these groups and spread a rhetoric expressive of group values (e.g. as McCulloch

1. A recent and comprehensive definition of an "interest group" is Joseph La Palombara's: "any aggregation of interacting individuals who manifest conscious desires concerning the authoritative allocation of values". *Interest Groups in Italian Politics* (Princeton: Princeton University Press, 1964), p. 18.

did for bullionism, Kelley for Careyite greenbackism, or Bland for silverite producerism); solidified these values into public policy (preeminently in silver demonetization in 1873); and thus kept faith with a projection of America's future that they and others believed in.

But other people, other groups, did not share significantly in the policy-making process. Shut out, they formed a rhetoric and program of their own, with which they attempted to replace the prevailing legislative orthodoxy—the outstanding case being the remonetization struggle of 1876-78. The money question was simply the visible, concrete policy issue around which group interests, ideology among them, were fought.

There is no space here to discuss group patterns at all fully, either the American ones or their foreign parallels, but perhaps it is still worth noting some of the most potent of them, even if they must be stripped of explanation.

Into 1873, the prevailing faith of policy-makers—people such as McCulloch, Boutwell, Sherman, Ruggles, Kasson, Knox, Linderman—was a more-or-less explicit utilitarian liberalism, a confidence in civilization, progress, science, natural law (especially the scientific, progressive, civilized natural laws of economics), whose policy manifestation was gold-monometallist bullionism. These views were very widely held by bankers, well-established manufacturers such as textile people, commercial interests (those in foreign trade being the most rigorous liberals of all economic groups), and those few agriculturists who expressed themselves on the money question. Sectionally they tended to be from the "better-informed" New York and New England area, from which the popular press and the political-economic textbooks emanated, supported by a scattering of Southern, Midwestern and West-coast voices, usually trading people. The only significant exception to the liberal orthodoxy held by this coalition was the producer philosophy bespoken by Careyite manufacturers and Midwestern laborites, whose policy objective was permanent inconvertibility for the greenback. But the greenbackers revered science, progress, nature, and civilization as much as the bullionists; they rejoiced in the existence, and stressed the necessity, of harmony among the elements of the society. Ideologically ecumenical, numerically small, and removed from administrative information and authority, the greenbackers were not in a position to affect policy significantly. The definition of the public interest held by Senator Sherman and the Secretaries of the Treasury, a definition that put gold monometallism, stable currency, and the integrity of the public credit foremost, prevailed without essential emendation.

It was otherwise after 1873. With the coming of depression, latent antagonisms among economic, sectional, and ideological groups became explicit. The National Labor Union, the fount of labor greenbackism, fell apart after the election of 1872; many formerly greenbackish manufacturers, shocked by depression-fed strikes and riots, fundamentally revised their self-image from that of producers whose natural allies were farmers and laborers to that of capitalists whose natural allies were other men of means such as bankers, merchants, and transporters. Greenbackism thus lost much of its pre-1873 group base. The remnants of labor greenbackism gained, however, a very numerous and potentially powerful ally: the previously silent agrarians. But partly because of many agrarians' predilection for some kind of "hard" money, partly because of the particular interests and beliefs of strategically placed Congressmen such as Bland and Kelley, this farmer-labor coalition, this new "union of the producing classes," considered free coinage of silver at least as desirable as greenbacks. These shifts in the affiliations of economic interest groups, above all the changed stances after 1873 of manufacturers and farmers, underlay the new and narrow rhetorics exemplified by Bland and Hewitt in 1876. The old notion of a harmony of interests gave way to polarities of capital against labor, creditors against debtors, manipulators against producers. "Limited" or "international" bimetallism, such as Sherman and Allison were advocating in 1876-78, became the outside limit of policy revision acceptable to the gold monometallists, while free silver began to replace greenback-ism as the softer-money policy most likely to be achieved on the currency question.

With the accomplishing of resumption and the return of better times in 1879, greenbackism became anachronistic (though it continued to attract votes for several years) and free silver became less urgent. The money question subsided as a policy issue. But rhetorical gongs and grapeshot were only put aside, not forgotten; when hard times returned about a decade later, they were employed again for the money fight that so preoccupied the 1890's. The pitched battle of interest group coalitions bearing their flaky rhetorical weapons finally came in the presidential election of 1896, when the Populist-Democrat William Jennings Bryan championed free silver against William McKinley and the Republican orthodoxy of international bimetallism. The defeat of Bryan signalled the defeat not only of free silver, but also of the money question itself as the policy issue manifesting the conflict of economic, ideological, and sectional groups within American society. The country then had to seek a more realistic way to deal with social change.

Meanwhile, international bimetallism (as something more than just a front for gold monometallism) fared little better than free silver. American policy-makers, responding to silver pressure, actually implemented the second Allison amendment to the Bland bill in 1878 and brought together an international monetary conference at Paris in that year to establish a worldwide gold-silver ratio. They received the coldest of cold shoulders. The economic and monetary developments of the seventies were having their effects on Europe as well as the United States. Bismarck fired his Liberal Finance Minister in 1876, began a policy of tariff protection, and lessened his faith in rigorous gold monometallism; the Third Republic denounced its free-trade Cobden-Chevalier treaty with Britain and dropped Napoleon's grandiose schemes for coinage unification based on the franc; Britain moved to strengthen her monetary ties with India and insulate the sterling area.

Economic liberalism was giving way to economic nationalism. Concurrently, the ideal of the Concert of Europe was losing ground to a pair of hostile alliance systems, as the "civilizing mission" of the West became Western imperialism. The gold standard, that stunted offspring of the old liberal world-view, ironically became the longest-lived of its progeny in Europe and America.

A Bibliographical
Review

RATHER THAN PROVIDE an exhaustive annotated bibliography of all of the primary and secondary sources used in this book, I think it will be more useful here to survey the most pertinent historical and economic writing on the subject. Footnotes, though they have been kept to a minimum, should provide sufficient direct reference to facts, observations, or opinions whose documentation, especially from primary sources such as manuscripts, public documents, and memoirs, seemed irreducible.

General Treatments, Chiefly Politically-oriented

In the whole span of American historical writing, few periods have been so excitingly studded with new interpretations based on extensive pioneering research, than the 1950's and '60's. Hardly a single important historical topic, from the early seventeenth century well into the twentieth, has escaped significant reformulation, with the result that American historiography has become one of the most rapidly changing areas of intellectual life. Amid this activity has been the revitalization of the history of the Reconstruction period. Historians and biographers such as Fawn Brodie, John and LaWanda Cox, John Hope Franklin, Harold Hyman, Eric McKitrick, Kenneth Stampp, Bernard Weisberger, C. Vann Woodward and a number of others, have dealt tellingly with Reconstruction in its customary sense, a postlude to the Civil War chiefly involving race relations, conditions in the South, and the restoration of the former Confederate states to the Union. But Reconstruction in that sense was over, except in a few scattered areas, well before 1877, as Franklin points out (*Reconstruction After the Civil War* [Chicago: University of Chicago Press, 1961], p. 196), and as a protean controversy it was over well before the end of the sixties (see present vol., p. 26).

The Reconstruction period as a prelude to the late nineteenth and early twentieth centuries, rather than as a postlude to the Civil War, had received substantially less attention from historians. Still, there did exist a prevailing interpretation: the view, advanced by Charles A. Beard and his wife Mary, and later by Howard K. Beale, that Reconstruction was part of a "Second American Revolution" by which Northeastern capitalists by law and deviousness fastened a tight economic grip on a prostrate South and pre-adolescent West. This view was killed in 1959 and since has been interred ever more deeply by the new vision and wide research into primary sources by some younger historians.

Journal articles in 1959 by Irwin Unger ("Business Men and Specie Resumption," *Political Science Quarterly*, LXXIV [March 1959], pp. 46-70) and Stanley Coben ("Northeastern Business and Radical Reconstruction: A Re-examination," *Mississippi Valley Historical Review*, XLVI [June 1959], pp. 69-90), and a slightly later article by Unger ("The Business Community and the Origins of the 1875 Resumption Act," *Business History Review*, XXXV [Summer 1961], pp. 247-62), significantly undermined the traditional viewpoint by demonstrating that the notion of a single "business" (as opposed to agrarian or labor) viewpoint on Reconstruction tariff and monetary policy, especially a hard-money viewpoint, was a fiction. Great disagreement existed among bankers, merchants, transporters, and manufacturers, depending on their product, marketing problems, location, and many other factors; so great was the diversity that, as Coben put it, "it seems clear that factors other than the economic interests of the Northeast must be used to explain the motivation and aims of Radical Reconstruction." Unger meanwhile showed that the critical Specie Resumption Act of 1875, so apparently a triumph of hard-money business interests, was really brought off by John Sherman and other legislators as a political compromise to re-unite the Republican Party on the money question in the face of great disagreement among its business and legislative supporters and in the threat of defeat in the election of 1876.

Another and very incisive reassessment of the Reconstruction money question appeared in 1959: Robert P. Sharkey's *Money, Class, & Party: an Economic Study of Civil War and Reconstruction* (Baltimore: The Johns Hopkins Press, 1959). Using manuscripts, government documents, printed recollections and contemporary treatises, delving deeply into pamphlet literature, newspapers, and the reports and publications of private organizations, Sharkey employed the interest-group approach to demonstrate the crudeness of Beard's business-versus-non-business polarity. The somnolence of farmers, the cross-purposes of financially oriented and industrially oriented businessmen, the fact that many Radicals were soft-money (even greenback) advocates and that they logically linked soft money and tariff protectionism, were among the many points Sharkey made.

Sharkey's book was a great step forward, both in his demolition of many of Beard's and Beale's conclusions and in his employment of largely ignored sources to do it. But there was still room for further scholarship. *Money, Class, & Party* could not be the last word on the Reconstruction money question if only because it stopped in 1869 and thus related the problem to the War that preceded it rather than to the social, economic, and political turmoil that followed. Furthermore, although it upended many of the Beard-Beale conclusions, it accepted their basic assumption that economic self-interest was the determining or at least pre-eminent motivator of events:

When the divergent interests of financial and industrial capitalists, of bankers and manufacturers are understood, the conceptual monolith of the interests of "capitalists" which the Beards have created falls to the ground, and it becomes apparent that the economic history of the Civil War and Reconstruction must be approached from the standpoint of the conflicting interests of various economic groups. . . .
[p. 300]

The first modern book to treat the Reconstruction money question as a unit, and which rejected not only the Beardian conclusions but the conceptual framework of economic interpretation, was Irwin Unger's *The Greenback Era: A Social and Political History of American Finance, 1865-1879* (Princeton: Princeton University Press, 1964). Unger, by employing the interest-group approach, found as had Coben and Sharkey that public policy rested not on a dualism of capitalists versus others or even of hard money versus soft, but on a sprawling pluralism of interests. But even more significantly, Unger realized that the effective interests were not just economic. Monetary doctrine (Carey, Sylvis and Andrew Cameron, Amasa Walker, many others, ideology ("Calvinism" versus "agrarianism"), private groups not overtly economic (the American Social Science Association, church groups, etc.), political exigency (e.g. the reasons behind the Specie Resumption Act), all played roles. The Pulitzer-Prize winner in history for 1964, *The Greenback Era* will stand for the foreseeable future as an authoritative description of the political history of the greenbacks and specie resumption and of the social groupings that shaped that political history. Unger's virtuous book did leave further work to be done: the rhetoric and ideology of the money question were more complicated than his dualism of Calvinism and agrarianism; he did not attempt to relate his story to the late nineteenth-century future; he dealt lightly with the pre-1876 phase of the silver question; and he did not explore the international aspects of the problem. Still, though *The Greenback Era* does not exhaust the subject or organize it in the only possible way, it has been decidedly the broadest and most thorough treatment to date.

Economic Histories

Economic historians have been recounting and analyzing the Reconstruction period ever since it happened. The present-day usefulness and reliability of their accounts varies enormously, but not especially according to the date of their appearance. Virtually all of those written before 1900, and too many of those written afterward, manifested a serene confidence in the eternal verity of the gold standard; they shared in, and helped perpetuate, the same economic orthodoxy which so influenced the policy-makers of the sixties and seventies. Because of this unrecognized bias their objectivity was short-circuited and they were in a poor position to produce an impartial or very profound account. As Bray Hammond once declared (*American Historical Review,* LXVII [October 1961], 15), "Something like an apostolic laying on of hands seems to have accompanied the sound money crusade, to which, from the Civil War to the New Deal, scholars lent themselves; and judgments expressed in the historical studies produced in that interval reflect the conventional sound-money convictions preached in the current political controversies, but now abandoned by all economists less than one hundred years of age." In the 1930's, Hammond continued, the old orthodoxy was not only shaken but stood on its head, when domestic specie payments were discarded once and for all in favor of inconvertible paper. One could add a further irony: silver, which pushed aside the greenback in the late seventies as the alternative to gold monometallism, fell of its own weight along with the bullionism on which it rested, and it was inconvertible paper that finally triumphed. Inconvertible paper, in fact, had not had spokesmen of any respectability since the last days of Henry C. Carey and Pennsylvania protectionism, and economic historians and economists almost to a man saw free-silver unlimited bimetallism as the threat to their cherished gold-standard orthodoxy. In the long view, however, what they were really fighting was an intramural battle within the bullionist camp.

The economic historiography begins with Henry R. Linderman's *Money and Legal Tender in the United States* (New York, 1878), and John Jay Knox's *United States Notes* (New York, 1884). As participants in the events, especially the demonetization process, Knox's and Linderman's books were not only treatises of the subjects in their titles, but also, not surprisingly, *pièces justificatives:* the 1873 Coinage Act simply wrote into law "what had been really," said Knox, "the unwritten law of the land for nearly forty years" (p. 151); though Linderman especially fell into revealing self-contradictions in places, their books were the beginnings of the "orthodox legend," the case for the defense.

Albert S. Bolles, who dedicated his *Financial History of the United States from 1861 to 1885* (New York, 1886) to President George F. Baker of the First National Bank of New York, contended that never in America, though often in Europe, was it policy-makers' intention to enhance gold values by demonetizing silver; the Public Credit Act of 1869, the refunding of 1870, and the 1873 silver demonetization were prudent and honest acts designed by the government to repay its creditors what they expected and deserved and to protect the public interest by dealing "liberally with its creditors . . . in order to sustain to the highest degree of efficiency its money-borrowing power." (p. 391).

In 1885 and in subsequent editions (especially at the peak of the money controversy of the nineties), J. Laurence Laughlin published his influential *History of Bimetallism in the United States* (New York, 1885, and later dates). Despite Laughlin's well-known connections with the anti-silver lobby in the nineties, he has been looked upon since as a quotable and citable authority, perhaps because he was an academic (Professor of Political Economy at the University of Chicago). Laughlin was at pains to show that silver was not really demonetized in 1873 by the Coinage Act, which was not conspiratorially produced, but rather in the revised statutes of 1874, which took away from silver its legal-tender power; there was no conspiracy, in other words, but if there was it happened in 1874, not 1873. Laughlin had no doubts, however, that the 1873 Act was something "for which we can not now be too thankful" (1888 edition, p. 93), for without it the 1879 resumption would have been in silver and all debts "would have been repudiated" to the extent of 15 percent.

In the nineties came William Harvey's popular (to the orthodox, insidious) *Coin's Financial School,* reiterating and spreading the agrarian legend of an anti-silver, anti-little man conspiracy in 1873; very quickly some rebuttals from Laughlin and others; and finally the first sober commentary on the subject: Willard Fisher's " 'Coin' and his Critics" (*Quarterly*

Journal of Economics, X [January 1896], pp. 187-208), which pointed out that the silver dollar was "dishonest" only in the sense that its bullion value was about half that of the gold dollar; it could just as logically be said, as the agrarians were doing, that gold was dishonest because it had appreciated. "Which of the two is dishonest can be determined only by long and difficult study," Fisher concluded. But people had no time for that in the campaign of 1896, and far fewer of them, no doubt, listened to Fisher than to Horace White, who stated in *Coin's Financial Fool,* his answer to Harvey, and more elaborately in his *Money and Banking* (Boston and London, 1896), that the 1873 demonetization had been public, in accord with the long-standing custom of the gold standard, and without any idea that silver would drop; in short, a forthright and timely statement of the orthodox legend. David K. Watson elaborated on this viewpoint in the edition of his *History of American Coinage* published in New York in 1899, and with the agrarian legend discredited along with Bryanism the orthodox legend was to have no serious challenge for years. It was substantially repeated in A. Barton Hepburn's *History of Coinage and Currency in the United States and the Perennial Contest for Sound Money* (New York, 1903), and in Alexander Dana Noyes' *Forty Years of American Finance* (New York and London, 1909).

By then, however, a generation had begun to write whose primary concern was economic-historical analysis rather than the defense of hard money in textbooks for the young or tracts for the public. First among these scholars was Wesley Clair Mitchell, with his *History of the Greenbacks, with Special Reference to the Economic Consequences of their Issue: 1862-65* (Chicago, 1903), and even sounder *Gold, Prices, and Wages under the Greenback Standard* (Berkeley, 1908). These pioneering works are still useful for establishing and relating trends in the gold premium and wholesale price indexes, for noting that the greenback was certainly not the only cause of the violent fluctuations of the period, especially since specie-paying foreign countries had problems too, and for showing how monetary fluctuations affected the various sectors of the economy differently. Warren M. Persons, Pierson M. Tuttle, and Edwin Frickey supplemented Mitchell's work by a closely written article contrasting post-Civil War and post-World War I economic conditions in America and comparing American trends with European ones ("Business and Financial Conditions following the Civil War in the United States," *Review of Economic Statistics* [Supplement; preliminary volume 2, 1920], pp. 1-55); F. D. Graham examined another dimension of the problem in "International Trade Under Depreciated Paper: The United States, 1862-79" (*Quarterly Journal of Economics,* XXXVI [February 1922], pp. 220-73), and Willard L. Thorp's *Business Annals* (New York, 1926) finally set forth systematically and succinctly the trends in economic and financial conditions in all of the major countries through the period and beyond. J. T. W. Newbold described the global secular trend in "The Beginnings of the World Crisis, 1873-96" (*Economic History* ["A Supplement to the *Economic Journal*"], II [1932], pp. 425-41), and with this there closed nearly three decades of economic-historical scholarship on the subject that in most important respects is still basic.

The hard-money bias was generally present but seldom jarring among the Mitchell-to-Newbold group. In the thirties, however, substantial scholarly progress was sometimes marred by a too-obvious awareness of contemporary controversy. Neil Carothers opened the decade with his *Fractional Money: A History of the Small Coins and Fractional Paper Currency of the United States* (New York, 1930), which discussed the origins of the silver question along with a great many other subjects beyond its narrow title; Carothers was well informed, aware as no previous author had been to the blindness of policy-makers as well as later legend-makers on both sides, but generally convinced that the country was lucky to have had the gold standard muddle through, despite what he saw as the clumsiness of Knox and others and their total unawareness that their 1873 Act abolished the bimetallic standard. Carothers' book is consequently often helpful, usually entertaining, but sometimes quite wrong—to say nothing more of his monometallist presuppositions. Close on Carothers' heels came

Don C. Barrett's *The Greenbacks and Resumption of Specie Payments, 1862-1879* (Cambridge, 1931), a curious throwback which defended the quantity theory of money and a rigorous hard-money viewpoint unflinchingly and without serious change from its exposition sixty-five years earlier by Secretary Hugh McCulloch. Then came Jeanette P. Nichols with "John Sherman: A Study in Inflation" (*Mississippi Valley Historical Review*, XXI [September 1934], pp. 181-94), and "John Sherman and the Silver Drive of 1877-78: The Origins of the Gigantic Subsidy" (*The Ohio State Archaeological and Historical Quarterly*, XLVI [April 1937], pp. 148-65), the first modern scholarship on the key personality of Sherman, yet reflecting some hard-money assumptions (inflation referred to greenbacks, the "gigantic subsidy" to the partial re-opening of the Mint to the silver of Western mining interests). William Shultz and M. R. Caine, in their textbook called *Financial Development of the United States* (New York, 1937), declared the 1873 Act by no means secret but certainly, in regard to its dropping of the silver dollar, not understood by Congress or public; Shultz and Caine oversimplified the matter less than any other writers before them and since, but they added little to an understanding of it. Finally in 1939 a renowned economist, Joseph Schumpeter, defended inconvertible paper in his *Business Cycles: A Theoretical, Historical, and Statistical Analysis of the Capitalist Process,* signalling that the long reign of gold-standard orthodoxy was substantially over. Still, the old faith persisted in textbooks, and none of them have dealt adequately with the origins of the silver question.

After World War II there appeared several research pieces that illuminated money-related aspects of the period: Samuel Rezneck's "Distress, Relief, and Discontent in the United States during the Depression of 1873-78" (*Journal of Political Economy*, LVIII [December 1950], pp. 494-512); the monumental study by Fritz Redlich, *Molding of American Banking: Men and Ideas* (New York, 1951); James K. Kindahl's "Economic Factors in Specie Resumption: the United States, 1865-79" (*Journal of Political Economy*, LXIX [February 1961], pp. 30-48), and his 1958 University of Chicago dissertation on the subject; *A Monetary History of the United States, 1867-1960,* by Milton Friedman and Anna Jacobson Schwartz (Princeton, 1963); and Richard H. Timberlake, Jr.'s "Ideological Factors in Specie Resumption and Treasury Policy *(Journal of Economic History,* XXIV [March 1964], pp. 29-52). By the time the last of these appeared, Paul M. O'Leary had suggested, in "The Scene of the Crime of 1873 Revisited: A Note" *(Journal of Political Economy,* LXVIII [August 1960], pp. 388-92), that Linderman and others were indeed aware since 1869 that silver would drop and had to be demonetized to preserve the monetary standard. The wheel had gone full circle; an academic article could aver that the silverite charge of foreknowledge and planning by policy-makers was true after all. O'Leary leaned heavily on Linderman's official report of 1872 and his book of 1877, and Friedman and Schwartz were not convinced that Linderman would have foreseen and acted on the decline in silver prices as early as 1869. (As chapter 5 of this book indicates, however, Linderman and others seem to have been working on such assumptions well before then.) The history of the question was by no means well understood even in the early 1960's: J. G. Gurley and E. S. Shaw still could say that the silver dollar was dropped in 1873 because it had not been circulating ("Money," in Seymour E. Harris, ed., *American Economic History* [New York, 1961], p. 113); Richard Hofstadter, in a long introduction to a new edition of Harvey's *Coin's Financial School* (Cambridge, 1963), depended too heavily on Laughlin and Carothers; and Paul S. Barnett's "The Crime of 1873 Re-examined" *(Agricultural History,* XXXVIII [July 1964], pp. 178-81) only reiterated some examples of the agrarian legend. But there had been great advances, most notably those of the Mitchell-to-Newbold generation of economists and by Coben, Sharkey, and Unger beginning in 1959.

International Aspects

There is a dearth of scholarly monographs on British, French, German, and other European developments relating to the money question, not only with regard to official policy itself but even more with regard to its social and intellectual dimensions such as, for example, interest groups. With the exception of a very few modern and well-researched items such as Edward F. Cox's "The Metric System: A Quarter-Century of Acceptance (1851-1876)" (*Osiris* [Bruges], XIII [1958], pp. 358-79), which describes the backdrop to the international coinage movement, or Ivo N. Lambi's *Free Trade and Protection in Germany, 1868-79* (Beiheft 44, *Vierteljahrschrift für Sozial- und Wirtschaftsgeschichte;* Wiesbaden, 1963), an extremely helpful analysis of the Bismarck Government's consequential shift from liberalism toward *Nationalökonomie,* one must rely mainly on general economic histories and the reports of contemporaries (as well as, of course, comparative economic studies such as those already mentioned).

Even the general histories (and I mention here only some of them) vary in usefulness. J. H. Clapham's *Economic Development of France and Germany, 1815-1914* (Cambridge, 1921) is a still reliable general treatment but says extremely little about money and monetary policy. The same is true of *Die Finanz- und Zollpolitik des Deutschen Reiches, nebst Ihren Beziehungen zu Landes- und Gemeinde-Finanzen, von der Gründung des Norddeutschen Bundes bis zur Gegenwart* (Jena, 1913), by Wilhelm Gerloff. On the other hand, Henry B. Russell's *International Monetary Conferences: Their Purposes, Character, and Results* (New York and London, 1898), though regrettably not annotated, is a rather full and helpful account of its subject, as is Henry Parker Willis' *History of the Latin Monetary Union: A Study of International Monetary Action* (Chicago, 1901). Frank A. Fetter's *Development of British Monetary Orthodoxy, 1797-1875* (Cambridge, 1965) helps explain the British tenacity for gold monometallism; Oswald Schneider's *Bismarcks Finanz- und Wirtschaftspolitik* (Munich and Leipzig, 1912) and A. Sartorius von Waltershausen's *Deutsche Wirtschaftsgeschichte, 1815-1914* (Jena, 1920) do give some idea of Prussian and German monetary developments.

But the testimony of contemporaries is almost as accessible and sometimes more helpful. The official documents of the French, British, and American governments, including commissions of investigation into the money question and reports of delegations to the 1867 and 1878 international monetary conferences, are first-rank sources. Ludwig Bamberger, the German Liberal leader whose influence on Bismarck was considerable until 1876, explained himself in *Reichsgold: Studien über Währung and Wechsel* (Leipzig, 1876). Walter Bagehot, the editor of the London *Economist,* left in book form *A Practical Plan for Assimilating the English and American Money, as a Step towards a Universal Money* (London, 1869) and *Some Articles on the Depreciation of Silver and on Topics Connected With It* (London, 1877), which represent prevalent British thinking. German semi-official opinion, especially Adolph Soetbeer's, may be found in the *Verhandlungen des Vierten Deutschen Handelstages zu Berlin vom 20 bis 23. Oktober 1868* (Berlin, 1868); that hard-working French monometallist and politician, M. Esquirou de Parieu, broke into print frequently but perhaps most revealingly in "Unification monétaire: réfutation des arguments de la minorité de la commission du Sénat des Etats-Unis" (*Journal des Economistes,* XIII [3d series; September 1868], pp. 420-23), and "Les Conférences Monétaires Internationales de 1867, et Leurs Résultats" (*Journal des Economistes,* XIII [3d series; February 1869], pp. 243-61). Léon Say, the French Minister of Finance through much of the seventies, published his views on the money question in volumes II and IV of his *Les Finances de la France Sous La Troisième République.* The principal expression of Louis Wolowski, France's most prominent bimetallic politician, is *L'Or et L'Argent* (Paris, 1870). A quite unfavorable view of American policy, from Switzerland's leading financial diplomat, is Charles Feer-Herzog, *La Conférence Monétaire Américaine, Tenue à Paris du 10 au 29 Août 1878: Rapport au Conseil Fédéral Suisse* (Berne, 1878). There are many other sources for European thought and policy, but these cover most of the main viewpoints.

Rhetoric and Ideology

Here too the modern literature is sparse and often no more accessible than important primary sources. Highly informative and deeply researched, the best general study for the period of the relation of ideas (especially political-economic ones) and government, is Sidney Fine's *Laissez Faire and the General-Welfare State: A Study of Conflict in American Thought 1865-1901* (Ann Arbor, 1956); Fine isolated "classical," "national," "historical," and "new" schools of political economy, described the sixties and seventies as having been dominated by the "classical" school, and is stimulating and informative although he did not sufficiently separate, in my opinion, classicists from Careyites, other producerites, or international bimetallists such as Francis Amasa Walker; for Fine the first real break in "classical" dominance came in the eighties through people such as Richard T. Ely and Simon Patten. Two other modern works, although they do not focus directly on monetary ideology, help greatly to establish the prevalence of natural law, producerism, and related beliefs of the time; these are *American Conservatism in the Age of Enterprise: A Study of William Graham Sumner, Stephen J. Field, and Andrew Carnegie,* by Robert G. McCloskey (Cambridge, 1951), and *Business in the Gilded Age: The Conservative's Balance Sheet* (Madison, 1952), by Edward C. Kirkland. Elie Halévy's *Growth of Philosophic Radicalism* (translated by Mary Morris; London, 1934) does not deal with the United States, but its relevance because of its treatment of utilitarianism has been noted (chapter 5 above).

Having noted those useful works, however, one reverts to primary sources. These are legion, but the following contain the main elements of the various schools. For bullionism and liberalism, which in policy terms practically always meant gold monometallism, see Francis Bowen, *American Political Economy: Including Strictures on the Management of the Currency and Finances since 1861* (New York, 1870), a popular textbook of the day; Samuel Hooper, *Currency or Money: its Nature and Uses, and the Effects of the Circulation of Bank-Notes for Currency* (Boston, 1855), by the man some called Boston's leading merchant and who had much to do with greenback, national bank, and silver demonetization legislation as a House Republican; Hugh McCulloch, *Our National and Financial Future* (the oft-cited "Fort Wayne Address" of 1865), wherein the Secretary set forth the moral and theoretical bases for his proposed policies; Simon Newcomb, *A Critical Examination of our Financial Policy During the Southern Rebellion* (New York, 1865), one of the most rigorous but influential contemporary statements; Amasa Walker, *The Science of Wealth: a Manual of Political Economy, embracing the Laws of Trade, Currency, and Finance* (Boston, 1866), an outstanding example of the treatment of political economy as a "moral science"; David A. Wells, *The Recent Financial, Industrial, and Commercial Experiences of the United States: A Curious Chapter in Politico-economic History* (2d edition; New York, 1872), a discussion of current events by a well-connected and well-regarded liberal, and Wells' *Robinson Crusoe's Money: or, the Remarkable Financial Fortunes and Misfortunes of a Remote Island Community* (New York, 1876), an early and good instance of anti-silver propaganda akin in spirit and typography to William Harvey's later pro-silver tract, *Coin's Financial School*.

International bimetallism is explained and advocated not only by Louis Wolowski (*L'Or et L'Argent,* noted previously), but by Henri Cernuschi's *The Bland Bill: Its Grounds, Its Alleged Dishonesty, Its Imperfections, Its Future* (Paris, 1878); by the Belgian, Emile Laveleye, in *Bi-Metallic Money* (translated by George Walker and published by the *Bankers' Magazine* of New York; New York, 1877); by the Londoner Ernest Seyd, most helpfully in his *magnum opus, Bullion and Foreign Exchanges Theoretically and Practically Considered; Followed by a Defence of the Double Valuation, with Special Reference to the Proposed System of Universal Coinage* (London, 1868), and *Suggestions in Reference to the Metallic Currency of the United States of America* (London, 1871); and in the United States most prominently, perhaps, by two men connected with the American delegation to the Paris International Monetary Conference of 1878, S. Dana Horton, in *Silver and Gold, and Their Relation to the Problem of Resumption* (Cincinnati, 1877), and Francis Amasa Walker, *International Bimetallism* (New York, 1896; first edition 1878).

The producer philosophy, Careyism, and their policy outcome in greenbackism are dealt with from various angles in, of course, Henry Charles Carey's works, such as his *Principles of Political Economy* (Philadelphia, 1857-58) and *Money: A Lecture Delivered before the New York Geographical and Statistical Society* (New York, 1857). Carey's nephew, Henry Carey Baird, updated and reapplied the master's thought in *Criticisms of the Recent Financial Policies of the United States and France: Including an Attempt to Explain the Cause of the Present Prostrate Conditions of the Southern States* (Philadelphia, 1875; the cause was not enough greenbacks). Carey's leading disciple in Congress, William D. Kelley, unburdened himself in *Speeches, Addresses and Letters on Industrial and Financial Questions* (Philadelphia, 1872), and in *Letters from Europe: Six Letters Written to the Philadelphia Times During the Summer of 1879,* which included an account of Kelley's interview with Bismarck, at which monetary policy was discussed. A Midwestern manufacturer, William A. Berkey, advocated greenbackism on Careyite grounds in *The Money Question: The Legal Tender Paper Monetary System of the United States* (Grand Rapids, 1876). The best place to find theoretical explanation and policy advocacy of greenbackism from the labor standpoint is in the editorials and articles in the organ of the National Labor Union, the *Workingman's Advocate,* published in the late sixties and the seventies in Cincinnati and Chicago. A very wide range of American opinion on the money question in the mid-seventies appeared in Senate Report 703 of the 44th Congress, 2d Session, *Report and Accompanying Documents of the United States Monetary Commission, Organized under Joint Resolution of August 15, 1876* (2 vols.; Washington, 1877 and 1879).

Index